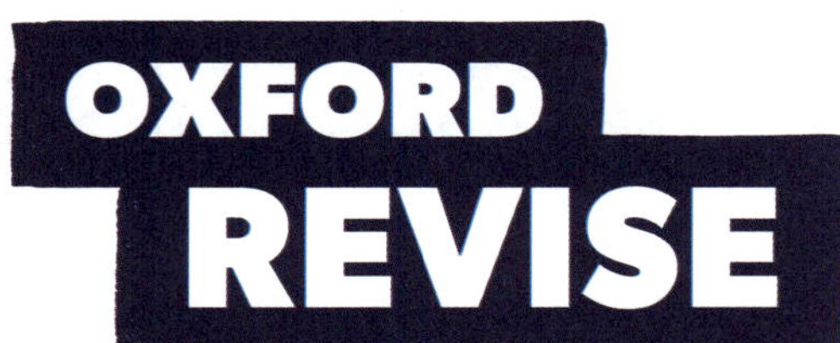

EDEXCEL GCSE

HISTORY

The USA, 1954–75: conflict at home and abroad

COMPLETE REVISION AND PRACTICE

Series Editor: Aaron Wilkes

Mark Stacey

Contents

Shade in each level of the circle as you feel more confident and ready for your exam.

How to use this book

This book uses a three-step approach to revision: **Knowledge**, **Retrieval**, and **Practice**. It is important that you do all three; they work together to make your revision effective.

Knowledge comes first. Each chapter starts with a **Knowledge Organiser**. These are clear easy-to-understand, concise summaries of the content that you need to know for your exam. The information is organised to show how one idea flows into the next so you can learn how everything is tied together, rather than lots of disconnected facts.

Answers and Glossary

You can scan the QR code at any time to access sample answers, mark schemes for all the exam-style questions, a glossary containing definitions of the key terms, as well as further revision support go.oup.com/OR/GCSE/Ed/Hist/USA

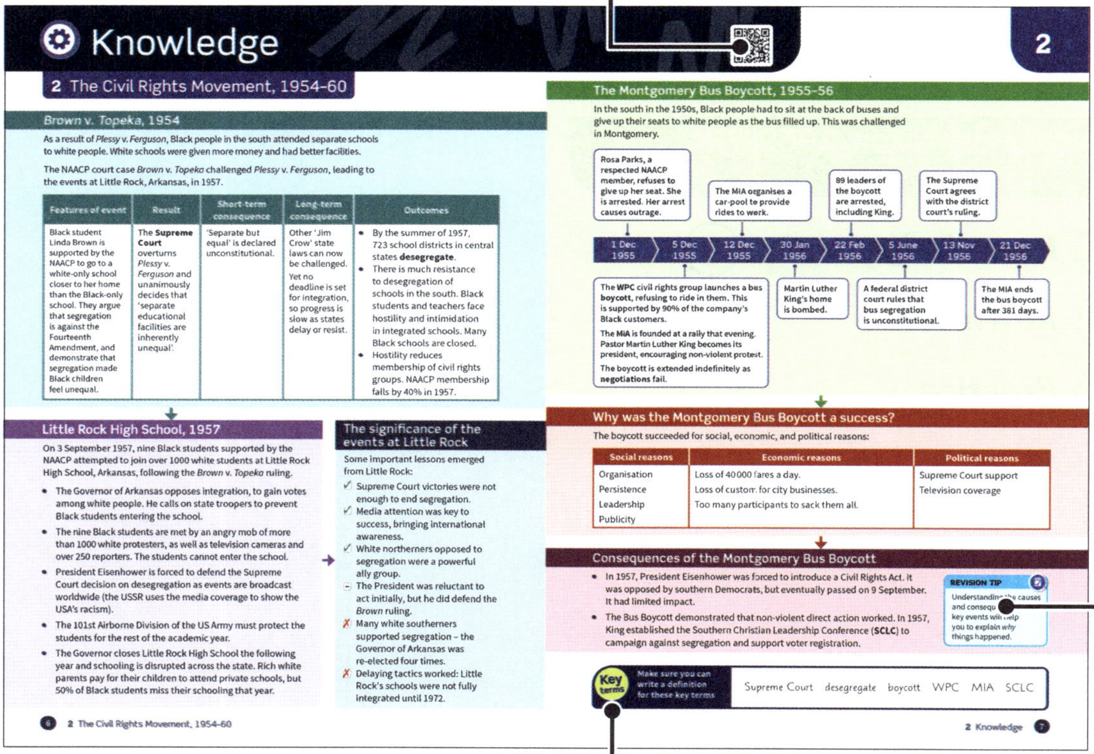

Knowledge

2

2 The Civil Rights Movement, 1954–60

Brown v. *Topeka*, 1954

As a result of *Plessy* v. *Ferguson*, Black people in the south attended separate schools to white people. White schools were given more money and had better facilities.

The NAACP court case *Brown* v. *Topeka* challenged *Plessy* v. *Ferguson*, leading to the events at Little Rock, Arkansas, in 1957.

Features of event	Result	Short-term consequence	Long-term consequence	Outcomes
Black student Linda Brown is supported by the NAACP to go to a white-only school closer to her home than the Black-only school. They argue that segregation is against the Fourteenth Amendment, and demonstrate that segregation made Black children feel unequal.	The **Supreme Court** overturns *Plessy* v. *Ferguson* and unanimously decides that 'separate educational facilities are inherently unequal'.	'Separate but equal' is declared unconstitutional.	Other 'Jim Crow' state laws can now be challenged. Yet no deadline is set for integration, so progress is slow as states delay or resist.	• By the summer of 1957, 723 school districts in central states **desegregate**. • There is much resistance to desegregation of schools in the south. Black students and teachers face hostility and intimidation in integrated schools. Many Black schools are closed. • Hostility reduces membership of civil rights groups. NAACP membership falls by 40% in 1957.

Little Rock High School, 1957

On 3 September 1957, nine Black students supported by the NAACP attempted to join over 1000 white students at Little Rock High School, Arkansas, following the *Brown* v. *Topeka* ruling.

- The Governor of Arkansas opposes integration, to gain votes among white people. He calls on state troopers to prevent Black students entering the school.
- The nine Black students are met by an angry mob of more than 1000 white protesters, as well as television cameras and over 250 reporters. The students cannot enter the school.
- President Eisenhower is forced to defend the Supreme Court decision on desegregation as events are broadcast worldwide (the USSR uses the media coverage to show the USA's racism).
- The 101st Airborne Division of the US Army must protect the students for the rest of the academic year.
- The Governor closes Little Rock High School the following year and schooling is disrupted across the state. Rich white parents pay for their children to attend private schools, but 50% of Black students miss their schooling that year.

The significance of the events at Little Rock

Some important lessons emerged from Little Rock:

- ✓ Supreme Court victories were not enough to end segregation.
- ✓ Media attention was key to success, bringing international awareness.
- ✓ White northerners opposed to segregation were a powerful ally group.
- – The President was reluctant to act initially, but he did defend the *Brown* ruling.
- ✗ Many white southerners supported segregation – the Governor of Arkansas was re-elected four times.
- ✗ Delaying tactics worked: Little Rock's schools were not fully integrated until 1972.

6 2 The Civil Rights Movement, 1954–60

The Montgomery Bus Boycott, 1955–56

In the south in the 1950s, Black people had to sit at the back of buses and give up their seats to white people as the bus filled up. This was challenged in Montgomery.

- 1 Dec 1955: Rosa Parks, a respected NAACP member, refuses to give up her seat. She is arrested. Her arrest causes outrage.
- 5 Dec 1955: The **WPC** civil rights group launches a bus **boycott**, refusing to ride in them. This is supported by 90% of the company's Black customers. The **MIA** is founded at a rally that evening. Pastor Martin Luther King becomes its president, encouraging non-violent protest. The boycott is extended indefinitely as **negotiations fail**.
- 12 Dec 1955: The MIA organises a car-pool to provide rides to work.
- 30 Jan 1956: Martin Luther King's home is bombed.
- 22 Feb 1956: 89 leaders of the boycott are arrested, including King.
- 5 June 1956: A federal district court rules that bus segregation is unconstitutional.
- 13 Nov 1956: The Supreme Court agrees with the district court's ruling.
- 21 Dec 1956: The MIA ends the bus boycott after 381 days.

Why was the Montgomery Bus Boycott a success?

The boycott succeeded for social, economic, and political reasons:

Social reasons	Economic reasons	Political reasons
Organisation	Loss of 40 000 fares a day.	Supreme Court support
Persistence	Loss of custom for city businesses.	Television coverage
Leadership	Too many participants to sack them all.	
Publicity		

Consequences of the Montgomery Bus Boycott

- In 1957, President Eisenhower was forced to introduce a Civil Rights Act. It was opposed by southern Democrats, but eventually passed on 9 September. It had limited impact.
- The Bus Boycott demonstrated that non-violent direct action worked. In 1957, King established the Southern Christian Leadership Conference (**SCLC**) to campaign against segregation and support voter registration.

REVISION TIP Understanding the causes and consequences of key events will help you to explain *why* things happened.

Key terms Make sure you can write a definition for these key terms: Supreme Court, desegregate, boycott, WPC, MIA, SCLC

2 Knowledge 7

Key terms Make sure you can write a definition for these key terms

The **Key terms** box highlights the key words and phrases that you need to know, remember and be able to use confidently.

REVISION TIP

Revision tips offer you helpful advice and guidance to aid your revision and help you to understand key concepts and remember them.

Retrieval

The **Retrieval questions** help you learn and quickly recall the information you've acquired. These are short questions and answers about the content in the Knowledge Organiser you have just reviewed. Cover up the answers with some paper and write down as many answers as you can from memory. Check back to the Knowledge Organiser for any you got wrong, then cover the answers and attempt all the questions again until you can answer *all* the questions correctly.

Make sure you revisit the Retrieval questions on different days to help them stick in your memory. You need to write down the answers each time, or say them out loud; otherwise it won't work.

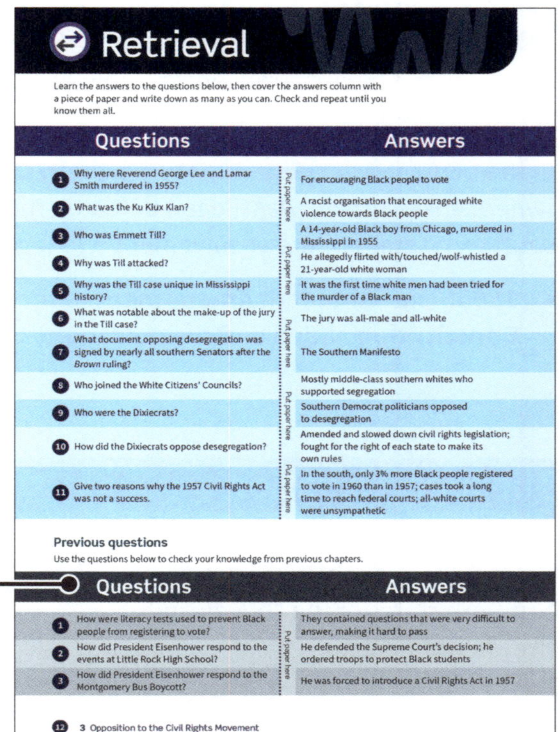

Retrieval

Learn the answers to the questions below, then cover the answers column with a piece of paper and write down as many as you can. Check and repeat until you know them all.

	Questions	Answers
1	Why were Reverend George Lee and Lamar Smith murdered in 1955?	For encouraging Black people to vote
2	What was the Ku Klux Klan?	A racist organisation that encouraged white violence towards Black people
3	Who was Emmett Till?	A 14-year-old Black boy from Chicago, murdered in Mississippi in 1955
4	Why was Till attacked?	He allegedly flirted with/touched/wolf-whistled a 21-year-old white woman
5	Why was the Till case unique in Mississippi history?	It was the first time white men had been tried for the murder of a Black man
6	What was notable about the make-up of the jury in the Till case?	The jury was all-male and all-white
7	What document opposing desegregation was signed by nearly all southern Senators after the *Brown* ruling?	The Southern Manifesto
8	Who joined the White Citizens' Councils?	Mostly middle-class southern whites who supported segregation
9	Who were the Dixiecrats?	Southern Democrat politicians opposed to desegregation
10	How did the Dixiecrats oppose desegregation?	Amended and slowed down civil rights legislation; fought for the right of each state to make its own rules
11	Give two reasons why the 1957 Civil Rights Act was not a success.	In the south, only 3% more Black people registered to vote in 1960 than in 1957; cases took a long time to reach federal courts; all-white courts were unsympathetic

Previous questions

Use the questions below to check your knowledge from previous chapters.

	Questions	Answers
1	How were literacy tests used to prevent Black people from registering to vote?	They contained questions that were very difficult to answer, making it hard to pass
2	How did President Eisenhower respond to the events at Little Rock High School?	He defended the Supreme Court's decision; he ordered troops to protect Black students
3	How did President Eisenhower respond to the Montgomery Bus Boycott?	He was forced to introduce a Civil Rights Act in 1957

12 3 Opposition to the Civil Rights Movement

Previous questions

Each chapter also has some **Retrieval questions** from **previous chapters**. Answer these to see if you can remember the content from the earlier chapters. If you get the answers wrong, go back and do the Retrieval questions for the earlier chapters again.

Practice

Once you think you know the Knowledge Organiser and Retrieval answers really well, you can move on to the final stage: **Practice**.

Each chapter has **Exam-style Questions** to help you apply all the knowledge you have learnt and can retrieve.

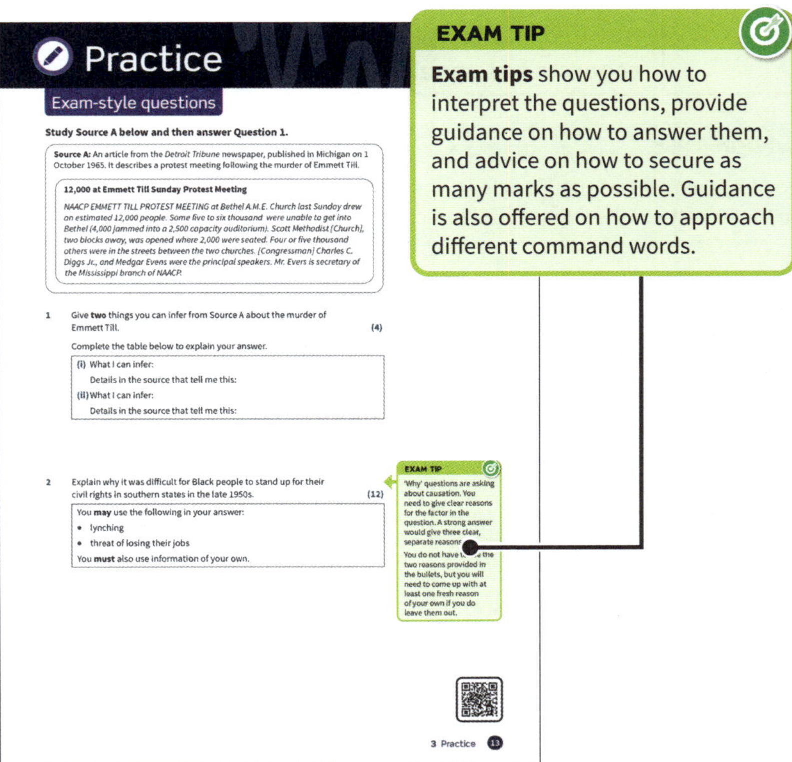

Practice

Exam-style questions

Study Source A below and then answer Question 1.

Source A: An article from the *Detroit Tribune* newspaper, published in Michigan on 1 October 1955. It describes a protest meeting following the murder of Emmett Till.

12,000 at Emmett Till Sunday Protest Meeting

NAACP EMMETT TILL PROTEST MEETING at Bethel A.M.E. Church last Sunday drew an estimated 12,000 people. Some five to six thousand were unable to get into Bethel (4,000 jammed into a 2,500 capacity auditorium). Scott Methodist [Church], two blocks away, was opened where 2,000 were seated. Four or five thousand others were in the streets between the two churches. [Congressman] Charles C. Diggs Jr., and Medgar Evens were the principal speakers. Mr. Evers is secretary of the Mississippi branch of NAACP.

1 Give **two** things you can infer from Source A about the murder of Emmett Till. **(4)**

Complete the table below to explain your answer.

(i) What I can infer:
Details in the source that tell me this:
(ii) What I can infer:
Details in the source that tell me this:

2 Explain why it was difficult for Black people to stand up for their civil rights in southern states in the late 1950s. **(12)**

You **may** use the following in your answer:
- lynching
- threat of losing their jobs

You **must** also use information of your own.

EXAM TIP

'Why' questions are asking about causation. You need to give clear reasons for the factor in the question. A strong answer would give three clear, separate reasons. You do not have to use the two reasons provided in the bullets, but you will need to come up with at least one fresh reason of your own if you do leave them out.

3 Practice 13

EXAM TIP

Exam tips show you how to interpret the questions, provide guidance on how to answer them, and advice on how to secure as many marks as possible. Guidance is also offered on how to approach different command words.

Knowledge

1 The lives of Black Americans in the early 1950s

The end of enslavement

Between 1525 and 1866, around 400 000 people were enslaved and forcibly transported from Africa to North America.

In the US Civil War (1861–65), the northern states (where enslavement was illegal) defeated the southern states (where enslavement was legal).

- **1865:** The Thirteenth **Amendment** to the **Constitution** ended enslavement in the USA.
- **1868:** The Fourteenth Amendment guaranteed all citizens 'equal protection of the laws'.
- **1870:** The Fifteenth Amendment guaranteed all citizens the right to vote.

Together, these amendments should have made all Americans equal, but Black people were still racially **discriminated** against socially, politically, and economically. Furthermore, Black Americans living in the north had a different experience from those living in the south.

The legal situation

Two key legal cases ensured discrimination against Black people was legal in the southern states of the USA, despite the amendments.

Case	Ruling
Dred Scott v. *Sandford* (1857)	All people of African descent, free or enslaved, were not US citizens.
Plessy v. *Ferguson* (1896)	It was legal to **segregate** white and Black people, provided facilities were '**separate but equal**'.

REVISION TIP

Knowing each amendment and legal case will help you to understand the subsequent topics.

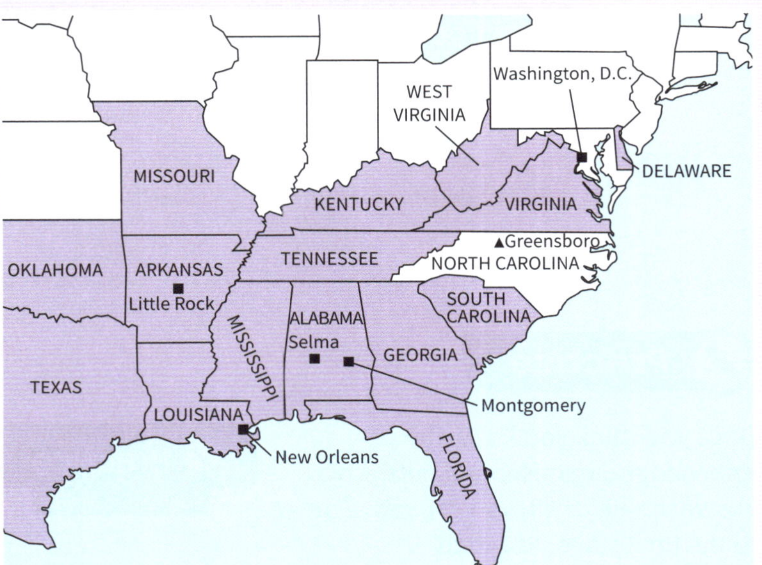

▲ *The southern states of the USA enforced segregation into the 1950s*

Voting rights in the south

Black people were a significant minority in many southern states. In Mississippi, for example, they made up 45% of the population in the 1950s.

'Jim Crow' state laws were used to prevent them from having their say:

- Grandfather clause: Black people (whose grandparents had been enslaved) were forced to apply to register to vote.
- Irregular opening times: This limited Black people's access to voter registration offices.
- Literacy test: Black people had to pass a test to register, which was deliberately made almost impossible to pass.
- Poll tax: Black people had to pay a tax before they could vote, which many could not afford.

Black people also faced threats of violence, intimidation, and being sacked if they voted. By 1964, only 6.7% of eligible Black people were registered to vote in Mississippi.

1

Comparing the north and the south in the early 1950s

Black people faced **prejudice** and discrimination to varying levels in both north and south:

	North	South
Jobs	Low-paid factory jobs. Service jobs in hotels/cafes.	Sharecroppers (tenant farmers). Domestic servants (such as maids and cooks).
	Lower wages than white people: 'last hired, first fired' if businesses struggled.	
Access to public facilities	Access was not segregated.	Access to schools, parks, beaches, cinemas, buses, waiting rooms, and restaurants was segregated; barred from attending universities.
Housing	Mostly lived in inner-city ghettoes (crowded, poorer areas).	Mostly lived in poor-quality houses on the edges of small, rural communities; blocked from moving to 'white areas' by landlords.
'Jim Crow' state laws	Did not apply.	Used extensively to prevent Black people from accessing their rights to vote and organise.
Relationship with police/army	Police officers and the legal system racially discriminated against Black people.	
	US Army was segregated until 1948; prejudice remained in both north and south.	

The work of civil rights organisations

Black people established **civil rights** organisations, such as the **NAACP** and **CORE**. Other local, business, and church organisations campaigned for civil rights, too.

NAACP (Founded 1909)	CORE (Founded 1942)
Tactics: Court cases to demonstrate that segregation was against the Constitution.	**Tactics: Non-violent direct action**, such as marches and **sit-ins**.
Membership: Black people and older, often middle-class, white people.	**Membership:** Black people and younger white people, often students.

There was some progress up to 1945, but social changes caused by the Second World War and the growth of the media paved the way for greater successes in the 1950s and 1960s:

- Over a million Black Americans fought during the war; they became determined to fight racism back home.
- By 1962, 90% of US households had a television.
- Newspaper daily sales grew by over 10 million between 1940 and 1950.

Make sure you can write a definition for these key terms

Amendment Constitution discriminated segregate separate but equal prejudice 'Jim Crow' state laws civil rights NAACP CORE tactics non-violent direct action sit-in

Retrieval

Learn the answers to the questions below, then cover the answers column with a piece of paper and write down as many as you can. Check and repeat until you know them all.

	Questions	Answers
1	What did the Thirteenth, Fourteenth, and Fifteenth Amendments to the US Constitution do?	Thirteenth: ended enslavement in the USA; Fourteenth: guaranteed 'equal protection of the laws'; Fifteenth: guaranteed all citizens the right to vote
2	Which key court case introduced the idea of 'separate but equal'?	*Plessy* v. *Ferguson* (1896)
3	Name three forms of discrimination faced by Black people in the south.	Three from: access to public facilities was segregated / barred from attending universities / state laws prevented Black people from voting / blocked from moving into 'white areas'
4	What did 'Jim Crow' state laws prevent?	They prevented Black people from accessing their rights to vote and organise
5	How were Black people treated by the police and the legal system?	Police officers and the legal system racially discriminated against Black people in both the north and south
6	How did the 'grandfather clause' prevent Black people from voting?	Black people (whose grandparents had been enslaved) had to register to vote, and registering to vote was made as difficult as possible
7	How were literacy tests used to prevent Black people from registering to vote?	They contained questions that were very difficult to answer, making it hard to pass
8	Black people made up what percentage of Mississippi's population in the 1950s?	45%
9	Which organisations campaigned for Black people's civil rights?	NAACP, CORE, local, businesses, and church organisations
10	What was the primary tactic the NAACP used in the fight for civil rights?	Legal action (court cases)
11	Which court case decided that all people of African descent, whether enslaved or free, could not be US citizens?	*Dred Scott* v. *Sandford* (1857)
12	What was CORE's primary tactic in the fight for civil rights?	Non-violent direct action
13	Which civil rights organisation consisted of a lot of students?	CORE
14	Around how many people were enslaved and forcibly transported from Africa to North America?	400 000
15	Until when was the US Army segregated?	1948

Put paper here

Practice

Exam-style questions

Study Source A below and then answer Question 1.

Source A: Protesters demonstrate against segregated education in Houston, Texas, in 1947

EXAM TIP

Before attempting to answer each question, use the 'BUG' method:

- **Box the command word**, so that you know what you are being asked to do.
- **Underline the key words** (the words that tell you which topic the question is about, and jog your memory about the topic).
- **Glance at the question again**, to pick up any additional information it is giving you and to help you picture what you need to do.

1 Give **two** things you can infer from Source A about the reasons why Black people demanded their civil rights. **(4)**

Complete the table below to explain your answer.

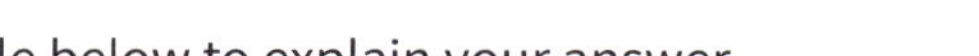

(i) What I can infer:
Details in the source that tell me this:
(ii) What I can infer:
Details in the source that tell me this:

SOURCE TIP

Remember, an inference is information you can extract from a source that is not directly stated, such as, information about emotions, attitudes, or significance.

Always back up your inference with evidence from the source in question, not from your own knowledge.

2 Explain why life was more difficult for Black people in the south than in the north in the early 1950s. **(12)**

You **may** use the following in your answer:
• access to public facilities
• 'Jim Crow' state laws.
You **must** also use information of your own.

Knowledge

2 The Civil Rights Movement, 1954–60

Brown v. *Topeka*, 1954

As a result of *Plessy* v. *Ferguson*, Black people in the south attended separate schools to white people. White schools were given more money and had better facilities.

The NAACP court case *Brown* v. *Topeka* challenged *Plessy* v. *Ferguson*, leading to the events at Little Rock, Arkansas, in 1957.

Features of event	Result	Short-term consequence	Long-term consequence	Outcomes
Black student Linda Brown is supported by the NAACP to go to a white-only school closer to her home than the Black-only school. They argue that segregation is against the Fourteenth Amendment, and demonstrate that segregation made Black children feel unequal.	The **Supreme Court** overturns *Plessy* v. *Ferguson* and unanimously decides that 'separate educational facilities are inherently unequal'.	'Separate but equal' is declared unconstitutional.	Other 'Jim Crow' state laws can now be challenged. Yet no deadline is set for integration, so progress is slow as states delay or resist.	• By the summer of 1957, 723 school districts in central states **desegregate**. • There is much resistance to desegregation of schools in the south. Black students and teachers face hostility and intimidation in integrated schools. Many Black schools are closed. • Hostility reduces membership of civil rights groups. NAACP membership falls by 40% in 1957.

Little Rock High School, 1957

On 3 September 1957, nine Black students supported by the NAACP attempted to join over 1000 white students at Little Rock High School, Arkansas, following the *Brown* v. *Topeka* ruling.

- The Governor of Arkansas opposes integration, to gain votes among white people. He calls on state troopers to prevent Black students entering the school.
- The nine Black students are met by an angry mob of more than 1000 white protesters, as well as television cameras and over 250 reporters. The students cannot enter the school.
- President Eisenhower is forced to defend the Supreme Court decision on desegregation as events are broadcast worldwide (the USSR uses the media coverage to show the USA's racism).
- The 101st Airborne Division of the US Army must protect the students for the rest of the academic year.
- The Governor closes Little Rock High School the following year and schooling is disrupted across the state. Rich white parents pay for their children to attend private schools, but 50% of Black students miss their schooling that year.

The significance of the events at Little Rock

Some important lessons emerged from Little Rock:

- ✓ Supreme Court victories were not enough to end segregation.
- ✓ Media attention was key to success, bringing international awareness.
- ✓ White northerners opposed to segregation were a powerful ally group.
- ⊟ The President was reluctant to act initially, but he did defend the *Brown* ruling.
- ✗ Many white southerners supported segregation – the Governor of Arkansas was re-elected four times.
- ✗ Delaying tactics worked: Little Rock's schools were not fully integrated until 1972.

The Montgomery Bus Boycott, 1955–56

In the south in the 1950s, Black people had to sit at the back of buses and give up their seats to white people as the bus filled up. This was challenged in Montgomery.

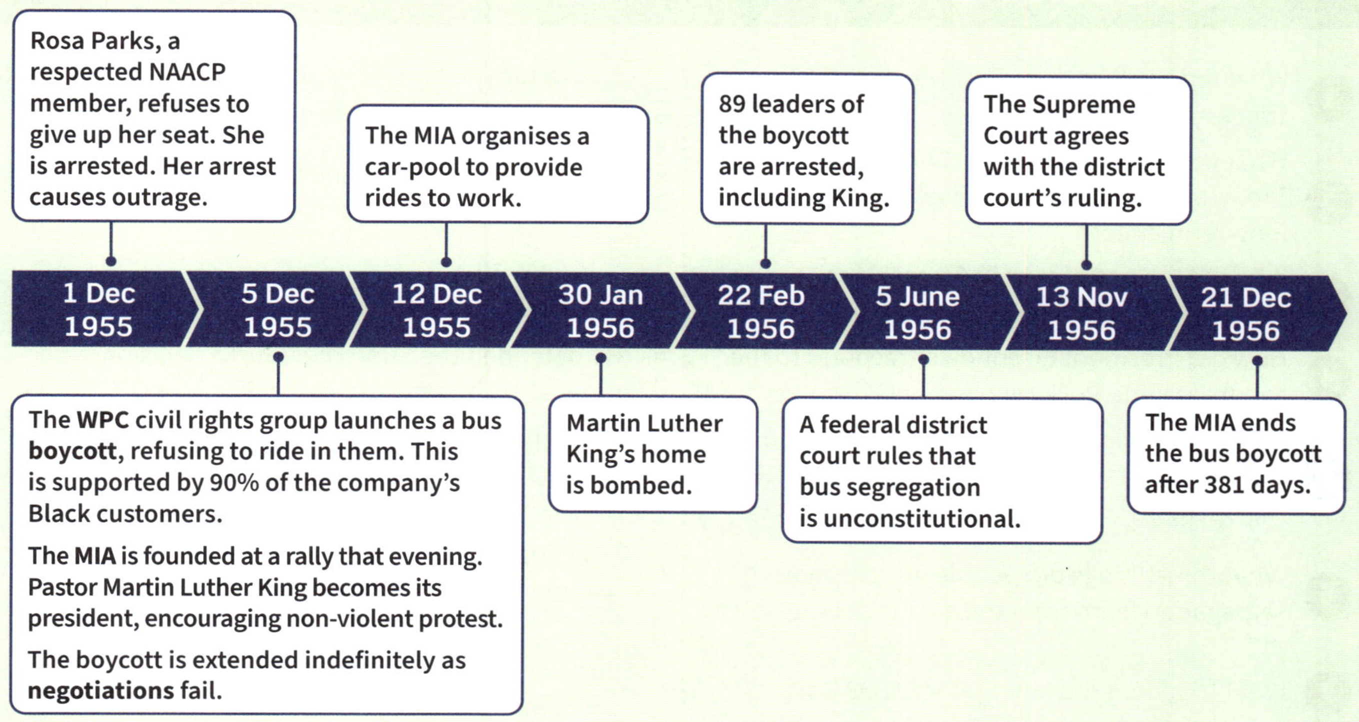

Why was the Montgomery Bus Boycott a success?

The boycott succeeded for social, economic, and political reasons:

Social reasons	Economic reasons	Political reasons
Organisation Persistence Leadership Publicity	Loss of 40 000 fares a day. Loss of custom for city businesses. Too many participants to sack them all.	Supreme Court support Television coverage

Consequences of the Montgomery Bus Boycott

- In 1957, President Eisenhower was forced to introduce a Civil Rights Act. It was opposed by southern Democrats, but eventually passed on 9 September. It had limited impact.
- The Bus Boycott demonstrated that non-violent direct action worked. In 1957, King established the Southern Christian Leadership Conference (**SCLC**) to campaign against segregation and support voter registration.

REVISION TIP

Understanding the causes and consequences of key events will help you to explain *why* things happened.

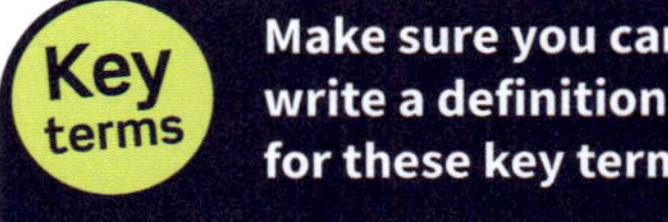

Make sure you can write a definition for these key terms

Supreme Court   desegregate   boycott   WPC   MIA   SCLC

Retrieval

Learn the answers to the questions below, then cover the answers column with a piece of paper and write down as many as you can. Check and repeat until you know them all.

	Questions	Answers
1	What did the Supreme Court decide in *Brown* v. *Topeka*, and in which year?	To overturn *Plessy* v. *Ferguson* (1896) because separate educational facilities were unequal; 1954
2	What did the Supreme Court fail to do in *Brown* v. *Topeka*, and what was the long-term effect?	It failed to give a deadline for integration, so progress was slow as states delayed or resisted
3	Why did the Governor of Arkansas oppose the integration of Little Rock High School?	To gain votes among racist white people
4	How did President Eisenhower respond to the events at Little Rock High School?	He defended the Supreme Court's decision; he ordered troops to protect Black students
5	What three things did people who opposed segregation learn from the events at Little Rock High School?	Supreme Court victories alone would not end segregation; media attention was vital; the support of white people in the north was important, too
6	What three things did people who supported segregation learn from the events at Little Rock?	Delaying tactics worked; many white southerners wanted segregation; Eisenhower was reluctant to act
7	What triggered the Montgomery Bus Boycott?	Rosa Parks refused to give up her seat on a bus for a white man, and was arrested; this caused outrage
8	How many days did the bus boycott last?	381
9	Name one economic reason why the Montgomery Bus Boycott was successful.	One from: loss of 40 000 bus fares a day / loss of custom for city businesses / too many participants to sack them all
10	How did President Eisenhower respond to the Montgomery Bus Boycott?	He was forced to introduce a Civil Rights Act in 1957
11	What organisation did Martin Luther King form after the success of the Boycott?	The Southern Christian Leadership Conference (SCLC)

Put paper here

Previous questions

Use the questions below to check your knowledge from previous chapters.

	Questions	Answers
1	Which key court case introduced the idea of 'separate but equal'?	*Plessy* v. *Ferguson* (1896)
2	What did 'Jim Crow' state laws prevent?	They prevented Black people from accessing their rights to vote and organise
3	Until when was the US Army segregated?	1948

Put paper here

Practice

Exam-style questions

Study Sources A and B.

1 How useful are Sources A and B for an enquiry into the importance of events at Little Rock in 1957? Explain your answer, using Sources A and B and your knowledge of the historical context. **(8)**

SOURCE TIP

The terms 'coloured', 'Blacks', and 'negro' were used by white Americans to refer to Black people unfavourably in this period. You can use them when quoting directly from the sources but should otherwise never use these terms as they are offensive. Refer to 'Black people' or 'African Americans' instead.

Source A: An adapted extract from the Supreme Court's decision in *Brown* v. *Topeka* (1954).

Segregation has a detrimental effect upon colored children. The impact is greater when it has the approval of the law, for the policy usually suggests the inferiority of the negro group. A sense of inferiority affects the motivation of a child to learn. Segregation, therefore, has a tendency to slow down the educational and mental development of negro children and to deprive them of some of the benefits they would receive in an integrated school system. In the field of public education, the doctrine of 'separate but equal' has no place. It is inherently unequal.

Source B: An adapted extract from the Southern Manifesto, a document signed by around 100 southern Democrats in 1956.

We regard the decision of the Supreme Court as a clear abuse of power. The original Constitution does not mention education. Neither does the 14th amendment nor any other amendment. This decision by the Court, contrary to the Constitution, is creating chaos and confusion in the south. It is destroying the friendly relations between the white and Negro races that have been created through 90 years of patient effort. It has planted hatred and suspicion where there has previously been friendship and understanding.

Study Interpretations 1 and 2. They give different views about the importance of events at Little Rock in 1957.

2 What is the main difference between these views? Explain your answer, using details from both interpretations. **(4)**

Interpretation 1: An adapted extract from a 2011 history book, *Cold War Civil Rights: Race and the Image of American Democracy*, by historian Mary Dudziak.

In Brown v. Topeka *(1954) the Supreme Court decided that school segregation was against the US Constitution. The Brown decision made it seem that the story American propaganda told was correct, that American democracy was based on principles of justice and equality. But the events in Little Rock threatened to undermine this story. As Little Rock became a massive worldwide news story, Eisenhower was forced to act. Each incident of discrimination reinforced the importance of race to US relations with predominantly black nations elsewhere in the world.*

Interpretation 2: An extract from a 1997 article called 'The Little Rock Crisis: Success or Failure for the NAACP?', by historian Adam Fairclough.

The Little Rock Crisis, followed by the Governor of Arkansas' triumphant re-election, killed the NAACP's hopes that school integration might be quick and painless. The two events revealed how great the white opposition to integration was. Southern politicians already knew that there were no votes to be won by supporting integration. They now saw that there were lots of votes to be won by appealing to the worst attitudes of white voters.

3 Suggest **one** reason why Interpretations 1 and 2 give different views about the importance of events at Little Rock in 1957. You may use Sources A and B to help explain your answer. **(4)**

4 How far do you agree with Interpretation 1 about the importance of events at Little Rock in 1957? Explain your answer, using both interpretations and your knowledge of the historical context. **(16)**

Knowledge

3 Opposition to the Civil Rights Movement

Southern racism and the Ku Klux Klan

Black people faced frequent violence and intimidation in the south at the hands of white racists, especially when campaigning or registering to vote.

- **Lynchings** happened across the south at the hands of mobs of white racists taking 'the law' into their own hands. Around 5000 lynchings were recorded between 1882 and 1968.
- In Mississippi in 1955, Reverend George Lee and Lamar Smith were murdered for encouraging Black people to vote. No one was arrested for either crime; Lee's shooting was filed as a car accident.

The racist organisation the **Ku Klux Klan** (KKK) was often behind the atrocities.

→ Racism was also found in white southern church organisations, where members were often members of the KKK.

→ The authorities usually looked the other way, because many police officers and judges were also members of the KKK.

Following the *Brown* v. *Topeka* Supreme Court decision, membership of the Ku Klux Klan increased to fight desegregation.

The Murder of Emmett Till, August 1955

Emmett Till was a 14-year-old Black boy from Chicago (in the north), who was visiting his cousins in the town of Money, Mississippi (in the south) in the summer of 1955.

▲ *Emmett Till*

Till visits a store in town, and allegedly flirts with, touches, or wolf-whistles at the owner's wife, a 21-year-old white woman.

→ 28 August: The store owner (Bryant) and his half-brother (Milam) go to Till's great-uncle's house, armed with a gun, and kidnap Till.

→ Several nights later, Till's body is found in a local river. He has been beaten, mutilated, and shot in the head. His body is barely recognisable.

→ Till's mother holds an open-casket funeral, saying: 'There was just no way I could describe what was in that box. No way. And I just wanted the world to see.'

→ Pictures of Till's body are published in local Black newspapers and picked up nationwide.

→ Bryant and Milam are arrested and charged with murder. It is the first time white men have been charged with the murder of a Black man in Mississippi.

→ 23 September: An all-white, all-male jury finds Bryant and Milam not guilty. Bryant and Milam later sell their story to a magazine for $3 500, sparking outrage.

The publicity created by Till's funeral caused anger across the USA and the world, feeding into the rapid growth of the Civil Rights Movement. However, Till's killers were never brought to justice.

Key terms **Make sure you can write a definition for these key terms**

lynching Ku Klux Klan manifesto White Citizens' Council Dixiecrat federal

Opposition to desegregation after *Brown* v. *Topeka*

The day of the *Brown* ruling became known as 'Black Monday' by many white southerners. It was followed by an extreme backlash against desegregation.

- The so-called 'Southern **Manifesto**', signed by 19 Senators on 12 March 1958, publicly rejected the *Brown* v. *Topeka* court ruling as illegal, claiming that desegregation was unconstitutional.
- Black families with children in integrated schools were threatened with violence, as were Black and white civil rights activists. Some schools were bombed.
- Some state governors promised to keep segregation: the Senator for Virginia called for 'massive resistance' and threatened desegregating schools with closure.
- In July 1954, the first **White Citizens' Council** (WCC) was set up, in Indianola, Mississippi. Many more WCCs appeared across the south, drawing greater middle-class membership than the KKK. By 1957, national membership of WCCs had reached around 250 000. The WCC threatened to sack Black workers and to use violence against them.
- Many local groups spring up to protest desegregation, often set up by white parents to threaten and intimidate Black people and their supporters.
- Many school boards find ways to resist desegregating, e.g. using admission tests to limit the number of Black students; using white protests as an excuse to exclude Black students 'for their own safety'.

Many Black people felt worse off after the *Brown* ruling than they had before: winning rights was one thing; enforcing them was another entirely. The NAACP and CORE worked with children in integrated schools to prepare them for the hostility they would face.

Political opposition to desegregation

Political opposition to desegregation occurred at both the local and state level.

- President Eisenhower was reluctant to force states to desegregate. He even spoke against the 1957 Civil Rights Act after reluctantly putting it forward.
- In the capital (Washington, D.C.), southern Senators and southern members of the House of Representatives in Congress used speeches and delaying tactics to block civil rights legislation, knowing that this would appeal to white voters.
- Southern Democrat politicians, known as '**Dixiecrats**', resisted by amending or slowing down civil rights legislation; there were too many Dixiecrats for their views to be ignored. Dixiecrats claimed they were not racist, but were fighting for the right of each state to make its own rules.
- 77 Southern Members of the House of Representatives signed the 'Southern Manifesto' in 1958 (see above).
- Judges and juries in the southern courts refused to convict white people of crimes against Black people and ignored Black-on-Black crimes. Black Americans could not serve on juries and there were no Black judges.

Features of the Civil Rights Act, 1957

The weaknesses of the 1957 Civil Rights Act showed the strength of opposition to it, and the difficulties of enforcing the law:

Features of the Civil Rights Act, 1957	Was it a success?
✓ Stated that all Americans had the right to vote. ✓ Allowed **federal** courts to prosecute when people were denied the right to vote. ✓ Six-member Commission to write a report on civil rights for the president.	✗ In the south, only 3% more Black Americans were registered to vote in 1960 than had voted in 1957. ✗ Cases took a long time to reach federal courts; few had been heard by 1965, and all-white courts were unsympathetic. ✗ Gathered information that contributed to later Acts.

Retrieval

Learn the answers to the questions below, then cover the answers column with a piece of paper and write down as many as you can. Check and repeat until you know them all.

	Questions	Answers
1	Why were Reverend George Lee and Lamar Smith murdered in 1955?	For encouraging Black people to vote
2	What was the Ku Klux Klan?	A racist organisation that encouraged white violence towards Black people
3	Who was Emmett Till?	A 14-year-old Black boy from Chicago, murdered in Mississippi in 1955
4	Why was Till attacked?	He allegedly flirted with/touched/wolf-whistled a 21-year-old white woman
5	Why was the Till case unique in Mississippi history?	It was the first time white men had been tried for the murder of a Black man
6	What was notable about the make-up of the jury in the Till case?	The jury was all-male and all-white
7	What document opposing desegregation was signed by nearly all southern Senators after the *Brown* ruling?	The Southern Manifesto
8	Who joined the White Citizens' Councils?	Mostly middle-class southern whites who supported segregation
9	Who were the Dixiecrats?	Southern Democrat politicians opposed to desegregation
10	How did the Dixiecrats oppose desegregation?	Amended and slowed down civil rights legislation; fought for the right of each state to make its own rules
11	Give two reasons why the 1957 Civil Rights Act was not a success.	In the south, only 3% more Black people registered to vote in 1960 than in 1957; cases took a long time to reach federal courts; all-white courts were unsympathetic

Put paper here

Previous questions

Use the questions below to check your knowledge from previous chapters.

	Questions	Answers
1	How were literacy tests used to prevent Black people from registering to vote?	They contained questions that were very difficult to answer, making it hard to pass
2	How did President Eisenhower respond to the events at Little Rock High School?	He defended the Supreme Court's decision; he ordered troops to protect Black students
3	How did President Eisenhower respond to the Montgomery Bus Boycott?	He was forced to introduce a Civil Rights Act in 1957

Put paper here

Practice

Exam-style questions

Study Source A below and then answer Question 1.

Source A: An article from the *Detroit Tribune* newspaper, published in Michigan on 1 October 1965. It describes a protest meeting following the murder of Emmett Till.

12,000 at Emmett Till Sunday Protest Meeting

NAACP EMMETT TILL PROTEST MEETING at Bethel A.M.E. Church last Sunday drew an estimated 12,000 people. Some five to six thousand were unable to get into Bethel (4,000 jammed into a 2,500 capacity auditorium). Scott Methodist [Church], two blocks away, was opened where 2,000 were seated. Four or five thousand others were in the streets between the two churches. [Congressman] Charles C. Diggs Jr., and Medgar Evens were the principal speakers. Mr. Evers is secretary of the Mississippi branch of NAACP.

1 Give **two** things you can infer from Source A about the murder of Emmett Till. **(4)**

Complete the table below to explain your answer.

(i) What I can infer:

Details in the source that tell me this:

(ii) What I can infer:

Details in the source that tell me this:

2 Explain why it was difficult for Black people to stand up for their civil rights in southern states in the late 1950s. **(12)**

You **may** use the following in your answer:

- lynching
- threat of losing their jobs

You **must** also use information of your own.

EXAM TIP

'Why' questions are asking about causation. You need to give clear reasons for the factor in the question. A strong answer would give three clear, separate reasons.

You do not have to use the two reasons provided in the bullets, but you will need to come up with at least one fresh reason of your own if you do leave them out.

4 The Civil Rights Movement, 1960–65

Greensboro and the sit-in movement, 1960

The next stage of the Civil Rights Movement involved students. They were willing to take greater risks, because they did not have families to look after or jobs that could be threatened by the White Citizens' Councils. Students were idealistic and willing to make sacrifices. They took matters into their own hands, first in Greensboro, North Carolina, sparking a widespread movement.

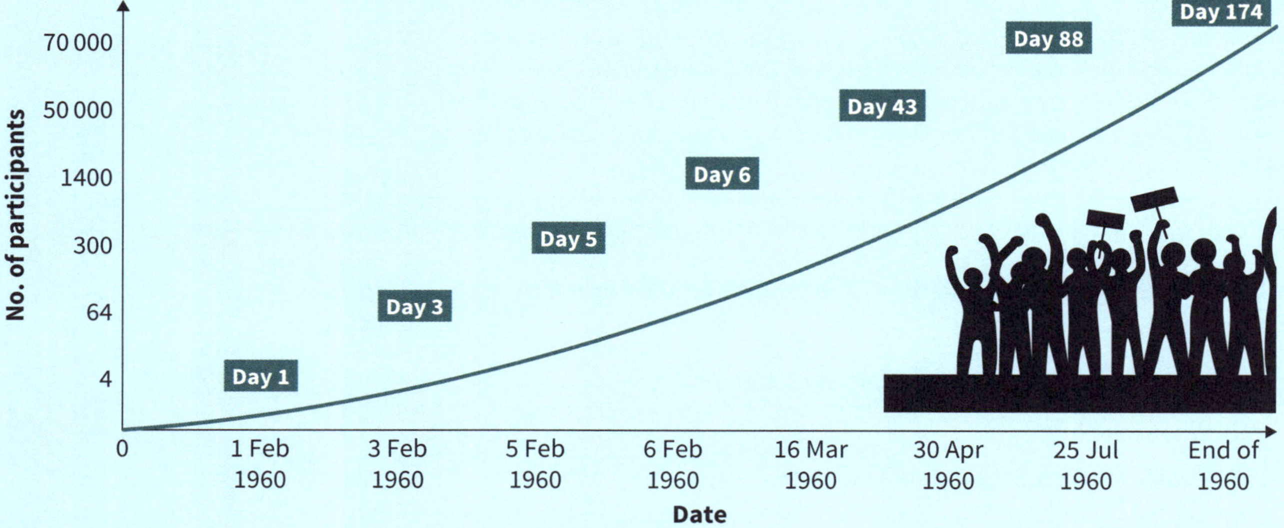

Day 1: Four Black college students ask to be served at a whites-only **lunch counter** in Greensboro, North Carolina. They are refused service and asked to leave. However, the students stay – without being served – until closing.

Day 3: The four students are joined by 60 others. None is served. They are threatened by some white customers.

Day 5: 300 students queue to sit at the lunch counter. As each one is removed by customers or police, another replaces them. Threats turn into assaults: coffee and ketchup are poured onto the students and cigarettes are stubbed out on them.

Day 6: 1400 protesters arrive at the store and are met by counter-protesters.

Day 43: President Eisenhower expresses concern over the ongoing protests, saying he is sympathetic to those striving to enjoy civil rights.

Day 88: Sit-ins spread to all the southern states (55 cities).

Day 174: The original lunch counter, at Woolworths in Greensboro, is desegregated; by this time the store has lost the equivalent of $1.8 million in today's money.

End of 1960: Over 70 000 people take part in sit-ins across the country.

Consequences of the sit-in movement

- The sit-ins attracted huge publicity because of the contrast between the non-violent patience of the protesters and the brutal treatment they faced from angry white customers. Once again, such racism made the USA look bad internationally and was used in anti-USA propaganda by the USSR.
- As the sit-in movement grew, volunteers from the NAACP and CORE helped with organisation and training.
- In April 1960, activist students involved with sit-ins formed their own group: the Student Nonviolent Coordinating Committee (**SNCC**), drawing on Martin Luther King's principles of non-violent protest.

lunch counter SNCC Freedom Ride

The Freedom Rides, 1961

Direct action had targeted schools, local buses, restaurants, and other public places. The next target was interstate travel.

- In the north, Black people on Greyhound buses could sit anywhere, but they had to move to the back when they reached the south.
- In December 1960, the Supreme Court ordered the desegregation of bus station facilities.
- In 1961, CORE decided to see if this had been carried out. Retrying an event from 1947, CORE launched a '**Freedom Ride**' from north to south.

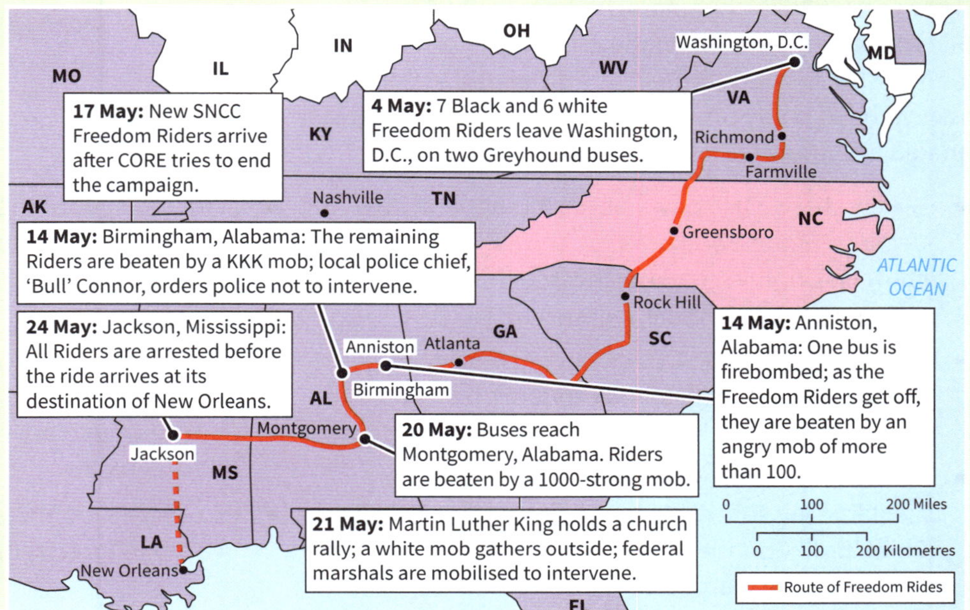

Consequences of the Freedom Rides

- Freedom Rides continued through the summer of 1961, with the same results.
- King appealed to Robert Kennedy, the Attorney General and brother of new Democrat President John F. Kennedy, but progress to protect the riders was slow.
- Over 300 Freedom Riders were arrested and imprisoned.
- On 1 November 1961, the government threatened to enforce desegregation laws if states did not comply.

REVISION TIP 

Consequences are key to explaining the significance – or importance – of events.

James Meredith and the University of Mississippi, 1962

In 1961, President Kennedy promised to be more proactive in supporting the Civil Rights Movement than Eisenhower had been. However, he had shown little support for the Freedom Riders. In 1962, Kennedy had a chance to make amends.

1961	1962	1962/3
Seven years after *Brown* v. *Topeka*, there are still no integrated schools in Mississippi. James Meredith, a Black American, applies to the University of Mississippi ('Ole Miss'). Meredith is rejected and takes the university to court, eventually reaching the Supreme Court.	**10 September:** The Supreme Court rules that Meredith must be admitted to the university. **30 September:** Meredith is physically prevented from registering by the university, so Kennedy orders over 500 federal marshals to the campus to enable him to do so. **1 October:** Marshals accompany Meredith through a crowd of 2500 protesters, who throw acid and Molotov cocktails (handmade petrol bombs). Two people are killed in the riot, including a French journalist, and several hundred are injured. Of the 300 people arrested, only 100 come from Mississippi.	Troops remain on campus with Meredith throughout his year-long course.

Knowledge

4 The Civil Rights Movement, 1960-65

The 1963 peace march in Birmingham, Alabama

The reaction in Birmingham, Alabama, when the Freedom Riders passed through, made this city an ideal target for King and the SCLC's new 'Project C'. This aimed to confront southern racism head on by provoking violence and gaining widespread media attention.

REVISION TIP 

It is important to try to remember factual details to add weight to your answers, such as just how many children were arrested.

- Birmingham was known as 'Bombingham' because of the frequent attacks on Black churches, homes, and businesses there. It remained completely segregated.
- On 3 April 1963, the SCLC began a campaign of sit-ins, protest marches, and economic boycotts. The SCLC encouraged children as young as five to march.
- Over 900 children were arrested, filling all the available jail space. King was also arrested. Police Chief 'Bull' Connor used police dogs and firehoses to disrupt the marches.
- Media images of the event were incredibly powerful and included TV footage of children's hands poking through the bars of the crowded jails.
- President Kennedy got involved, saying that these events had 'damaged America'. Talks began, Connor was removed, and the city agreed to desegregate.
- Pro-segregation reactions forced Kennedy to send in 3000 federal troops.

The 1963 'March on Washington for Jobs and Freedom'

Martin Luther King planned a centenary march to celebrate the passing of the Thirteenth Amendment, to highlight the lack of progress in civil rights both economically and politically.

Significance of the March on Washington, 1963

- 28 August: 250 000 people march on Washington from across the country (around a quarter of the participants are white).
- The SCLC, SNCC, NAACP, and CORE are involved in the planning.
- Over 3000 journalists from all over the world cover the march.
- Around 50 US celebrities join the marchers, including Sammy Davis Jr, Bob Dylan, Joan Baez, James Baldwin, and Marlon Brando.
- King makes a powerful speech about his 'dream' of equality, confirming him as the spokesman of the Civil Rights Movement.

King's leadership

Many saw King's leadership as central to the success of the Civil Rights Movement:

- ✓ educated
- ✓ Christian values
- ✓ non-violent
- ✓ passionate and charismatic speaker

▲ *King addresses the crowd at the March on Washington, 28 August 1963*

Freedom Summer, 1964

In June 1964, the *New York Times* ran an article entitled 'Mississippi: A Profile of the Nation's Most Segregated State'. In Mississippi in 1964, 'Jim Crow' state laws still existed and only 7% of the Black population (about 40% of the state population) were eligible to vote.

The SNCC and CORE therefore made Mississippi a key target for their campaigns.

- Volunteers taught people how to pass literacy tests and supported 17 000 Black Mississippians in attempting to register to vote. Only 1600 were accepted.
- The Mississippi Freedom Democratic Party (MFDP) and 30 Freedom Schools were established, all run by volunteers.
- Volunteers were mostly students, Black and white. They received training on dealing with harassment, arrests, imprisonment, and abuse.
- On 21 June 1964, three volunteers disappeared. Police in Neshoba County, Mississippi, failed to investigate and the FBI was called in. The bodies of the three young men were found on 4 August. They had been murdered by members of the local KKK.

Kennedy, Johnson, and the Civil Rights Act, 1964

After promising support in his election campaign, Kennedy introduced his Civil Rights Act in 1963. However, it faced the same opposition as Eisenhower's Act in 1957.

- On 22 November 1963, President Kennedy was assassinated in Dallas, Texas, and his Vice President, Lyndon B. Johnson, replaced him.
- Kennedy's assassination allowed Johnson to present the Civil Rights Act as Kennedy's 'legacy', making it much more difficult for the Dixiecrats to dilute the legislation. It passed by 290 votes to 130.

The 1964 Civil Rights Act:

- ✓ banned segregation in all public spaces
- ✓ banned job discrimination
- ✓ was enforced by a new Equal Opportunities Commission
- ✗ did not *explicitly* ban voter discrimination in individual states.

Selma, 1965

The 1964 Civil Rights Act was a huge step forward, but it failed to protect voting rights. The SCLC worked with the SNCC in Selma, Alabama, to help tackle this. Selma had fewer white people than Black people, but it had the lowest rate of Black voter registration in Alabama.

By this time, King was at the height of his fame and influence: in 1964, he had been named *TIME* magazine's 'Man of the Year' and been awarded a Nobel Peace Prize.

- The campaign featured sit-ins and boycotts.
- On 7 March 1965, 600 protesters tried to march from Selma to Montgomery (the state capital) to present a petition to the Governor of Alabama. The petition demanded protection for Black voting rights.
- King expected the Selma Police Chief to react violently, resulting in increased media exposure.
- Police stopped the march, tear-gassed the protesters, and beat them with clubs. The event became known as 'Bloody Sunday'.
- Johnson brought in the National Guard to support the marchers.
- Ten days later, 25 000 people completed the march and presented the petition.

The Voting Rights Act, 1965

Johnson reacted to Selma by passing the Voting Rights Act in August 1965.

Nearly 250 000 new Black voters registered that year and numbers continued to increase rapidly.

The 1965 Voting Rights Act:

- ✓ outlawed literacy tests and poll taxes as ways of deciding who could vote
- ✓ enabled federal officials to monitor voter registration instead of state officials.

Retrieval

Learn the answers to the questions below, then cover the answers column with a piece of paper and write down as many as you can. Check and repeat until you know them all.

Questions	Answers
1 Where did the 1960 sit-ins begin?	Greensboro, North Carolina
2 Which group was formed during the sit-ins?	Student Nonviolent Coordinating Committee (SNCC)
3 What kind of bus journeys did the Freedom Riders go on?	Interstate bus journeys (as opposed to local buses)
4 How did opponents of desegregation try to disrupt the Freedom Rides?	Firebombed the bus at Anniston; dragged Riders off buses and beat them; beat them when the buses stopped; Riders were arrested
5 How many protectors and protesters were present when James Meredith tried to register at 'Ole Miss'?	Over 500 federal marshals to protect him, and 2500 protesters
6 What was Birmingham, Alabama's nickname and why?	'Bombingham', because of the frequent attacks on Black churches, homes, and businesses there
7 How many children were arrested during the Birmingham campaign?	Over 900
8 Why did the 1963 march on Washington gain significant press attention?	There were 250 000 marchers; celebrities took part; it was on the anniversary of the Thirteenth Amendment; King's famous 'I have a dream' speech
9 Why was Mississippi targeted in the Freedom Summer?	It was seen as the most segregated state; only 7% of the Black population were registered to vote
10 Which President passed the Civil Rights Act, and in which year?	Lyndon B. Johnson in 1964
11 Why did the SCLC try to organise a campaign in Selma?	Selma was predominantly Black but had the lowest rate of Black voter registration in Alabama
12 How effective was the Voting Rights Act of 1965?	Very. Almost 250 000 extra Black people were registered to vote by the end of 1965

Put paper here

Previous questions

Use the questions below to check your knowledge from previous chapters.

Questions	Answers
1 How many days did the bus boycott last?	381
2 What was the Ku Klux Klan?	A racist organisation that encouraged violence towards Black people
3 Who were the Dixiecrats?	Southern Democrat politicians opposed to desegregation

Put paper here

Practice

Exam-style questions

Study Sources A and B.

1 How useful are Sources A and B for an enquiry into the importance of the different participants in the fight for civil rights in Mississippi in the years 1961 to 1962? Explain your answer, using Sources A and B and your knowledge of the historical context. **(8)**

Source A: An extract from a statement made by Attorney General Robert Kennedy on 24 May 1961.

> *Very difficult conditions now exist in the states of Mississippi and Alabama. Besides the groups of 'Freedom Riders' travelling through these states, there are curiosity seekers, publicity seekers, and others who are seeking to serve their own causes, as well as many persons who are travelling because they must use the interstate carriers to reach their destination. In this confused situation, there is an increasing possibility that innocent persons may be injured. A mob asks no questions. A cooling off period is needed.*

Source B: An extract from a radio speech by Democratic Governor of Mississippi Ross Barnett on 13 September 1962, shortly before James Meredith tried to register at the University of Mississippi.

> *Even now ... professional agitators and the unfriendly liberal press and other trouble makers are pouring across our borders intent upon instigating strife among our people. Paid propagandists are continually hammering away at us in the hope that they can succeed in bringing about a division among us. Every effort is being made to intimidate us into submission to the tyranny of judicial oppression. The Kennedy Administration is lending the power of the federal government to the ruthless demands of these agitators.*

Study Interpretations 1 and 2. They give different views about the importance of the different participants in the fight for civil rights in Mississippi in the years 1961 to 1962.

2 What is the main difference between these views? Explain your answer, using details from both interpretations. **(4)**

Interpretation 1: University of Mississippi historian William H. Doherty quoted in *'The Fight for Men's Minds': The Aftermath of the Ole Miss Riot of 1962* by Charles W. Eagles (2009).

> *In 1973 Doherty criticised the moral failure of participants in 1962 and the 'bland journalists and historians' who judged events in terms of politics and not morality. Though he also criticised James Meredith for 'undue individualism' and ignorance of the larger Civil Rights Movement, Doherty agreed that Meredith 'did nothing immoral' and had given a 'heroic solo performance.' Doherty reserved his harshest judgement for state and national leaders. He blamed the Kennedys for failing to understand Mississippi, its leaders, and the political pressures on the university.*

Interpretation 2: Adapted from *A Thousand Days: John F. Kennedy in the White House* by Arthur M. Schlesinger, Jr (1965).

> *Though some American Negroes felt Kennedy might have acted sooner this was quickly forgotten as they watched him send the Army to aid the admission of Meredith. In the autumn elections the Democrats won more Negro votes than ever. Then on November 20 Kennedy finally issued the executive order on housing. it marked a new step toward equal opportunity. In the middle of 1963, when a poll asked Negroes who had done most for Negro rights, the first three were the NAACP, Martin Luther King, Jr, and President Kennedy.*

3 Suggest **one** reason why Interpretations 1 and 2 give different views about the importance of the different participants in the fight for civil rights in Mississippi in the years 1961 to 1962. You may use Sources A and B to help explain your answer. **(4)**

4 How far do you agree with Interpretation 1 about the importance of the different participants in the fight for civil rights in Mississippi in the years 1961 to 1962? Explain your answer, using both interpretations and your knowledge of the historical context. **(16)**

Knowledge

5 Malcolm X and Black Power

The Civil Rights Movement in the north

The Civil Rights Movement is often associated with the south; however, in the north, Black people still faced many problems:

- They could vote, but often lived in the poorest areas of cities (ghettoes).
- It was difficult for Black people to get a good education and good jobs.

The rise of Malcolm X and the Black Power movement saw a shift in focus towards these issues.

Malcolm X

Born: Malcolm Little in 1925. He later rejected his 'slave' surname and used 'X'.

Parents: Father murdered by white racists; mother sent to a psychiatric hospital.

▲ *Malcolm X*

- Whilst in prison for burglary, he joined the **Nation of Islam** (NOI), a **militant** organisation influenced by Islam and **Black nationalism**.
- In a 1959 TV interview, he called white people 'collectively' evil.
- He expressed contempt for King and the idea of non-violence, echoing a growing belief that these methods had failed: inequality was clear to see in the ghettoes.
- He encouraged Black people to be proud of their identity and to defend themselves 'by any means necessary' against white attacks.
- NOI's membership grew to 30 000 members by 1963, at least in part due to his passionate campaigns. However, he became disillusioned with NOI and left in 1964, thereafter adopting a more tolerant, less militant outlook.
- He founded his own religious organisation – Muslim Mosque, Inc. (MMI) – as well as the Organization of Afro-American Unity (OAAU) to work with other civil rights organisations.
- He was assassinated by members of the NOI whilst giving a speech on 21 February 1965. Over 15 000 people paid their respects after his funeral.

The emergence of Black Power

Black people found a new way to express their anger with the emergence of the **Black Power** movement. Members talked of a social revolution to improve the lives of Black people in the USA.

Beliefs and ideas

- pride in Black heritage
- rejected white support
- against forced integration
- militant language
- influenced by Malcom X.

→

Reasons for growth

- popularity of Malcom X
- 'failure' of Civil Rights Movement/Civil Rights Acts
- ongoing discrimination
- shift of focus away from civil rights onto social issues/Vietnam War
- call for Black people to have pride and stand up for their rights.

→

Results

- focused on local issues, e.g. forcing companies to hire Black workers
- campaigns were often successful
- widespread media coverage, e.g. Stokely Carmichael and 1968 Mexico Olympics.

Stokely Carmichael

Encouraging Black people to register to vote was one step. The next step was deciding who they should vote for.

▲ *Stokely Carmichael*

- In 1965, SNCC member Stokely Carmichael set up the Lowndes County Freedom Organization as a party to represent Black Americans; its symbol was a panther.
- In 1966, Carmichael was elected **Chair** of the SNCC. He encouraged supporters of Black Power to join and launched SNCC campaigns in the northern ghettoes.
- During the 1966 'March Against Fear', led by 'Ole Miss' student James Meredith, Carmichael made militant speeches and coined the phrase 'Black Power', which led many campaigners to adopt his more **radical** beliefs.
- In 1968, Carmichael left the SNCC. He was made honorary Prime Minister of the Black Panther Party in 1969.

The 1968 Mexico Olympics

Black Power appeared on the world stage at the 1968 Olympic Games in Mexico.

▲ *US athletes Tommie Smith (centre) and John Carlos (right) give the Black Power salute at their medal ceremony, at the 1968 Olympic Games*

- During the US national anthem, two Black American medal-winners bowed their heads and raised an arm, each showing a black gloved fist: the salute used by many Black Power groups.
- Boos rang around the stadium and both athletes were suspended by the US Olympic team – but the Black Power salute became famous worldwide.
- Many young people were inspired to join the Black Power movement or adopt its more confrontational tactics.

The Black Panthers

The Black Panther Party for Self-Defense was formed in California in October 1966. It became one of the largest and most notorious of the Black Power groups.

It behaved like a political party, with a ten-point programme of demands, and a military visual style of black trousers, black leather jacket, top, and beret.	Members followed the police around in predominantly Black areas, and called for Black officials and police officers to serve Black communities.
Members gained media attention by marching to the state Capitol building carrying guns to protest a law banning people from carrying guns openly.	The Party carried out social work and campaigns, set up clinics on health, legal rights, and education, and had free breakfast programmes.
The Party demanded an end to police brutality against Black Americans, freedom for Black prisoners, and equal employment, housing, and education.	Members' intimidating appearance and demands made them a target for confrontations with the police and FBI infiltration, so the Party's influence rapidly declined.

Key terms Make sure you can write a definition for these key terms

Nation of Islam   militant
Black nationalism   Black Power
Chair   radical

REVISION TIP

You may see different interpretations of groups like the Black Panthers, some focusing on their provocative acts and others on their good works.

Retrieval

Learn the answers to the questions below, then cover the answers column with a piece of paper and write down as many as you can. Check and repeat until you know them all.

	Questions	Answers
1	Which organisation did Malcolm X join whilst in prison?	The Nation of Islam (NOI)
2	How were Malcolm X's views different to King's?	Malcolm X rejected non-violence, believing that white people were 'collectively' evil
3	What happened on 21 February 1965?	Malcolm X was assassinated by members of the Nation of Islam
4	Which organisation did Stokely Carmichael chair?	SNCC
5	What does 'Black Power' mean?	Black people should be proud of their heritage and stand up for themselves without white help
6	Why was the 1968 Mexico Olympics significant for the idea of 'Black Power'?	Two Black athletes gave the Black Power salute when receiving their medals, gaining widespread media attention for the cause
7	When and where was the Black Panther Party formed?	October 1966, California
8	What was the full name of the Black Panthers?	The Black Panther Party for Self-Defense
9	What social programmes did the Black Panthers set up?	Clinics to advise on health, legal rights, and education; free breakfast programmes
10	Which organisations targeted the Black Panthers?	The police and the FBI
11	Why did some view the Black Panthers as intimidating?	They wore black, military-style uniforms, carried guns, and challenged the police

Put paper here

Put paper here

Put paper here

Put paper here

Previous questions

Use the questions below to check your knowledge from previous chapters.

	Questions	Answers
1	What triggered the Montgomery Bus Boycott?	Rosa Parks refused to give up her seat on a bus for a white man, and was arrested; this caused outrage
2	How did opponents of desegregation try to disrupt the Freedom Rides?	Firebombed the bus at Anniston; dragged Riders off buses and beat them; beat them when the buses stopped; Riders were arrested
3	Why did the SCLC try to organise a campaign in Selma?	Selma was predominantly Black but had the lowest rate of Black voter registration in Alabama

Put paper here

Practice

Exam-style questions

Study Source A below and then answer Question 1.

Source A: Huey Newton, one of the founders of the Black Panthers, posing for a photograph in 1968 wearing the uniform adopted by the group.

SOURCE TIP

You should scrutinise visual sources as thoroughly as written sources. It is inaccurate to dismiss cartoons as exaggerated, drawings as made-up, and to accept photographs as 100% reliable. Use your contextual knowledge and study the details depicted carefully before answering any visual source-based questions.

1 Give **two** things you can infer from Source A about the Black Panther Party. **(4)**

Complete the table below to explain your answer.

(i) What I can infer:
Details in the source that tell me this:
(ii) What I can infer:
Details in the source that tell me this:

2 Explain why the Black Power movement became popular. **(12)**

You **may** use the following in your answer: • slow progress in the campaign for civil rights • Malcolm X You **must** also use information of your own.

EXAM TIP

Don't just describe the society or situation in the question; be sure to *explain why*. Consider how social, economic, political, and cultural factors led to the result described in the question. One way to do this is to look for short-term triggers, medium- and long-term reasons, and link them together.

Knowledge

6 The Civil Rights Movement, 1965–75

The riots of 1965–68

Growing frustration among Black people that their economic situation was not improving boiled over from 1964. Riots in cities across the USA occurred due to unemployment and poor housing, combined with the uncompromising language of Black Power.

From 1964 to 1968, there were over 500 separate riots, in which:

- almost 200 people lost their lives, and thousands were injured
- over a billion dollars of property damage was recorded by insurance companies.

	1964	1965	1966	1967	1968
Riots	11	11	53	158	289
No. days	34	20	109	408	739
Killed	2	35	11	83	66
Injured	996	1,132	525	2,801	5,302
Arrested	2,917	4,219	5,107	17,011	31,680
Arson attacks	238	3,006	812	4,627	6,041

▲ *1964–68 riot statistics, compiled by Robert Margo, ResearchGate*

There were four major riots:

- In New York City in July 1964, police triggered one by shooting a young Black man, two weeks after the Civil Rights Act and the month after the Mississippi murders.
- After Selma, a violent arrest sparked another riot in Los Angeles in August 1965.
- Major riots followed in Chicago and Cleveland (1966), and Newark and Detroit (1967).

1 Police action

- Rioting was often triggered by police action: police shot 65 Black people (27 in the back, 25 unarmed) between 1963 and the 1965 Los Angeles riot.

2 Local responses

- Within local communities, there were minor attacks on white properties (e.g. stores that discriminated).
- Over 80% of participants were young Black men.

3 Escalating violence

- Attacks led to increased violence and looting.
- There were casualties, both Black and white, but most were Black people shot by white police officers or soldiers.

4 Restoring order

- The military was brought in to restore order.
- Reforms were promised; King and the SCLC, and President Johnson, agreed on the need for action.

The Kerner Report, 1968

In July 1967, President Johnson ordered an enquiry to investigate the causes of the riots.

In February 1968, the Kerner Report concluded that: 'Our nation is moving toward two societies, one Black, one white – separate and unequal.'

Over two million Americans bought copies of the report.

The Kerner Report:

- blamed 'white racism' for the riots
- criticised unfair police treatment and brutality for worsening the riots
- accused the media of exaggerating the scale of the riots
- stated that the government needed to listen to Black communities, and provide more aid to repair the damage done by racism.

King's campaign in the north

After the success of the 1965 Voting Rights Act, King decided to focus the SCLC on working towards economic rights for urban Black people.

1966	*January*: King announces the Chicago Freedom Movement to show that non-violence can still work. It targets housing and jobs.	Demonstrations and marches start to build momentum.
	July: A major riot breaks out, damaging King's position.	Later marches target all-white areas, but the public is much less supportive. Marchers are met by violence and hostility.
	August: The Mayor of Chicago reaches an agreement with King about housing.	The Chicago Freedom Movement is largely unsuccessful. The agreement is ignored.
1967	King plans the Poor People's Campaign, in Washington, D.C., for all people – Black or white.	
1968	*4 April*: King is assassinated by James Earl Ray, a white man, on his hotel balcony.	Rioting in 200 towns across the USA, with 40 killed, thousands injured, and 27 000 arrests in five days.
	11 April: A Civil Rights Act is rapidly passed, covering housing, civil rights workers, and increasing punishments for rioting.	White support for the Civil Rights Movement declines due to Black Power, the severity of the riots, and a perception that the fight has been won.
	19 June: The Poor People's Campaign marches to Washington.	The campaign fails. The SCLC leadership and protesters argue.
1969	The SNCC drops 'non-violent' from its name.	The SNCC loses many original members.

The extent of progress in civil rights by 1975

Nixon replaced Johnson as President in 1969. Although he occasionally spoke up for civil rights, he tried to appeal to a '**silent majority**' in the south and north who wanted an end to civil rights protest.

Considerable progress had been made by the Civil Rights Movement by 1975. However, life in the USA was still profoundly different for Black Americans compared to white Americans.

Political rights by 1975	Economic rights by 1975	Social rights by 1975
✓ Black and white Americans had the same political rights, protected by federal law. ✓ 15 Black members of Congress. ✓ Cities such as Newark, Detroit, Los Angeles and Washington had Black mayors. ✓ The 1970 Voting Rights Act banned literacy tests. ✗ The percentage of elected Black officials was still not close to the percentage of Black people in the country.	✓ Nixon encouraged Black businesses and home ownership. ✓ More middle-class Black Americans. ✓ Black Americans closed the gap in average pay. ✗ Black people twice as likely to be unemployed. ✗ The average Black household had only 60% of the income of the average white household. ✗ Black Americans were three times more likely to live in poverty.	✓ The *New York Times* declared 'The South's public schools are now the most desegregated in the country'. ✓ 'Jim Crow' state laws had been abolished across the USA. ✗ Life expectancy for Black people was five years less than for white people. ✗ More Black university graduates, but white people were twice as likely to hold a degree. ✗ In 1972, almost two-thirds of Black children were in majority-Black schools.

Retrieval

Learn the answers to the questions below, then cover the answers column with a piece of paper and write down as many as you can. Check and repeat until you know them all.

	Questions	Answers
1	Where did major riots occur during 1964–68?	New York; Los Angeles; Chicago/Cleveland; Newark/ Detroit
2	What was a common trigger for the 1960s race riots?	Police action: US police shot 65 Black people between 1963 and the 1965 Los Angeles riot
3	When was the Kerner Report published?	February 1968
4	What did the Kerner Report conclude?	That the USA was 'moving towards two societies, one Black, one white – separate and unequal'
5	Which campaigns did King plan in 1966 and 1967, and which cities did they focus on?	1966: the Chicago Freedom Movement, Chicago; 1967: the Poor People's Campaign, Washington, D.C.
6	What happened after King's assassination?	Rioting in 200 towns across the USA, with 40 killed, thousands injured, and 27 000 arrests in five days
7	What key areas did the 1968 Civil Rights Act address?	Housing, workers' civil rights, and punishments for rioting
8	How did the riots impact support for the Civil Rights Movement?	They reduced support for the Civil Rights Movement, particularly from white Americans
9	How many Black members of Congress had been elected by 1975?	15
10	How comparable were the poverty rates for Black and white Americans by 1975?	Black Americans were three times more likely to live in poverty
11	How many Black children were still in majority-Black schools in 1972?	Almost two-thirds

Put paper here

Previous questions

Use the questions below to check your knowledge from previous chapters.

	Questions	Answers
1	What did the Supreme Court decide in *Brown* v. *Topeka*, and in which year?	To overturn *Plessy* v. *Ferguson* (1896) because separate educational facilities were unequal; 1954
2	Why was Mississippi targeted in the Freedom Summer?	It was seen as the most segregated state; only 7% of the Black population were registered to vote
3	How were Malcolm X's views different to King's?	Malcolm X rejected non-violence, believing that white people were 'collectively' evil

Put paper here

Practice

Exam-style questions

Study Sources A and B.

1 How useful are Sources A and B for an enquiry into the importance of Martin Luther King to the campaign for civil rights in the north USA? Explain your answer, using Sources A and B and your knowledge of the historical context. **(8)**

Source A: Stokely Carmichael speaking at the University of California, Berkeley, 29 October 1966, to an audience of 14 000 people.

Source B: From an interview given in 1989 by Albert Raby of the Coordinating Council of Community Organizations of Chicago.

... the movement was at a low ebb when we invited Dr. King to come to Chicago. ...his, promise to come was re-energizing to the movement. Ah, it created, brought back the coalition in the city, and I think reactivated us all. ... we had dissipated I think, most of our energy at that point. ... it re-energized the entire movement and allowed us to come back, ah, as a coalition, to form around him, and to start again.

Study Interpretations 1 and 2. They give different views about the importance of Martin Luther King to the campaign for civil rights in the north USA.

2 What is the main difference between these views? Explain your answer, using details from both interpretations. **(4)**

EXAM TIP

It is not enough to simply state a difference. In order to reach the higher level, you must show how the interpretations support your answer.

Interpretation 1: An adapted extract from *The Civil Rights Movement* by historian Mark Newman, published in 2004.

King agreed with Carmichael that blacks needed to develop group strength and achieve bargaining power. King also regarded the ghettoes as internal colonies exploited by white capitalists. King's increasing radicalism developed from his shocked realisation that racism deeply pervaded the entire nation, and from his opposition to the Vietnam War.

Interpretation 2: An adapted extract from *The American Dream* by historian Esmond Wright, published in 1996.

By the late 1960s, organizations such as the NAACP, King's SCLC, and SNCC faced increasingly strong challenges from new militant organizations. The Panthers' strategy of 'picking up the gun' reflected the feelings of many inner city blacks. A series of major 'riots' erupted during the last half of the 1960s as civil rights reforms did not address the problems faced by millions of poor blacks.

3 Suggest **one** reason why Interpretations 1 and 2 give different views about the importance of Martin Luther King to the campaign for civil rights in the north USA. You may use Sources A and B to help explain your answer. **(4)**

4 How far do you agree with Interpretation 2 about the importance of Martin Luther King to the campaign for civil rights in the north USA? Explain your answer, using both interpretations and your knowledge of the historical context. **(16)**

7 Reasons for US military involvement in Vietnam, 1954–63

Control of Vietnam

Vietnam is a small country in southeast Asia that had a big impact on the USA in the 1960s and 1970s. The USA also had a big impact on Vietnam.

Before that time, Vietnam had been controlled by different countries, leading to war there.

Prior to 1940	During the Second World War	After 1945
Vietnam kingdoms become part of the French Empire in Asia, known as French Indochina.	• Japan captures Vietnam in 1940. • Leader Ho Chi Minh forms the Vietminh, a left-wing group, to fight for an independent Vietnam.	• France tries to reclaim Vietnam. • The Vietminh resist, using **guerrilla** tactics, leading to a nine-year war with France. • Communist China supports the Vietminh. • The USA supports France. By 1954, the USA is paying 80% of France's war costs.

The end of French rule in Vietnam

- Between March and May 1954, French and Vietminh forces fought in the Battle of Dien Bien Phu.
- The battle ended in defeat for the French, and they were forced to leave Vietnam.
- France asked the USA for help.

The division of Vietnam

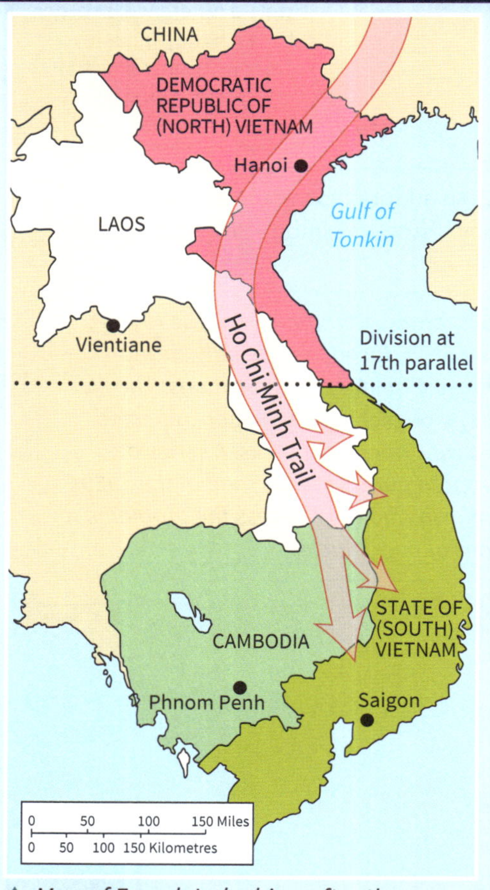

▲ *Map of French Indochina after the Geneva Accords, July 1954*

After the French defeat, a conference was organised in Geneva in 1954 to sort out the situation. Representatives from Vietnam, France, China, the UK, the USA, and the USSR attended.

The agreements reached at the Geneva Conference were summarised in ten documents known as the Geneva Accords:

- French Indochina would be split into four independent countries (see map): Laos, Cambodia, the Democratic Republic of (North) Vietnam, and the State of (South) Vietnam.
- Vietnam would be divided at the 17th parallel.
- The pro-communist Vietminh would control the northern Democratic Republic of Vietnam under President Ho Chi Minh.
- An anti-communist government under Ngo Dinh Diem would control the southern State of Vietnam. (Diem was Catholic; Vietnam was mostly Buddhist.)
- After two years, elections would reunite the country.

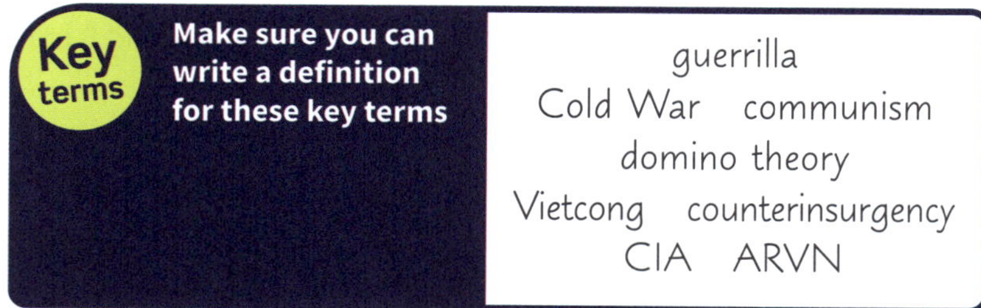

Reasons for greater US involvement in Vietnam under Eisenhower

After the Second World War, the USA engaged in a **Cold War** against **communism**.

- Ho Chi Minh was popular and the USA feared that he could win the democratic elections for the Vietminh.
- The Vietminh was influenced by communism from the USSR and Russia. The US government saw communism as a dangerous ideology that would spread to other Asian countries. This was known as the **domino theory** (countries would fall to communism, one after the other, like a row of dominoes).
- The US government gave money and military support to Diem's government to try to stop communism spreading. It also sent advisers to train the State of (South) Vietnam's military.
- Both Eisenhower and Kennedy wanted to appear 'tough on communism'.

Diem's government

Backed by the USA, Diem refused to hold the elections promised in 1956. His government became increasingly corrupt and less democratic.

- In October 1955, US officials supported fixed elections to confirm Diem's position.
- Diem's government took advantage of US support to treat opponents brutally and get rich from US aid (about $1.5 billion between 1954 and 1960), neglecting the poor lower classes.
- Anger and resentment built in South Vietnam, particularly as Buddhists were persecuted.
- Protests started against Diem, and opposition to his regime increased.
- In 1957, 65 000 suspected communists were arrested and 2000 were killed. Revenge attacks targeted Diem's officials.
- The Vietminh established the **Vietcong** in South Vietnam: guerrilla soldiers funded by the North to bring down Diem's government and unite the whole country.
- In May 1959, with Chinese backing, the Vietminh sent military aid to the Vietcong.

Reasons for greater US involvement in Vietnam under Kennedy

By early 1961, over half of South Vietnam was under the control of the 12 000 Vietcong.

President Kennedy increased US involvement in Vietnam to support **counterinsurgency** measures.

As a result of the 'Strategic Hamlet Program', Vietcong membership tripled between 1962 and 1964.

1. Kennedy wants to be seen as 'tough on communism', as his election victory in 1960 was very close.
2. Kennedy increases support to South Vietnam from 700 US military advisers to 16 000 by the end of 1963, and financial support by around $40 million.
3. Kennedy supports Diem's 'Strategic Hamlet Program', moving peasants into new fortified villages in areas under the control of the **ARVN** (Army of the Republic of Vietnam).
4. Kennedy instructs the **CIA** to help with the 'Strategic Hamlet Program', but it is very unpopular with peasants.
5. Diem's unpopularity in the South is clear. The CIA encourages Diem's generals to lead a coup against him. Diem is arrested and shot in November 1963.

Retrieval

Learn the answers to the questions below, then cover the answers column with a piece of paper and write down as many as you can. Check and repeat until you know them all.

	Questions	Answers
1	Which two countries controlled Indochina in the first half of the twentieth century?	France and Japan
2	In which battle did the Vietminh defeat the French, leading to the French withdrawal?	Battle of Dien Bien Phu
3	Who was the leader of the Vietminh and first President of North Vietnam?	Ho Chi Minh
4	Who was the leader of South Vietnam after the partition of the country in 1954?	Ngo Dinh Diem
5	What was the domino theory?	The US belief that if one country became communist others nearby would follow, one after the other, like a row of dominoes
6	Why did Kennedy take a more aggressive approach to Vietnam than Eisenhower had?	Kennedy had won a close election in 1960 and wanted to show that he was 'tough on communism'
7	What was the 'Strategic Hamlet Program'?	A State of Vietnam policy supported by Kennedy and the CIA, which moved peasants into new fortified villages in areas controlled by the ARVN
8	How did Kennedy escalate the US presence in Vietnam?	He increased support for Diem's regime from 700 military advisers to 16 000 and increased funding by around $40 million
9	What happened to Diem in November 1963?	He was removed by his own generals in a coup encouraged by the CIA, arrested, and shot dead
10	What was the impact of the 'Strategic Hamlet Program'?	It was very unpopular and, as a result, Vietcong membership tripled within three years

Put paper here

Previous questions

Use the questions below to check your knowledge from previous chapters.

	Questions	Answers
1	What was CORE's primary tactic in the fight for civil rights?	Non-violent direct action
2	How were Black people treated by the police and the legal system?	Police officers and the legal system racially discriminated against Black people in both the north and south
3	What key areas did the 1968 Civil Rights Act address?	Housing, workers' civil rights, and punishments for rioting

Put paper here

Exam-style questions

Study Source A below and then answer Question 1.

Source A: Vietnamese Buddhist monk Thích Quảng Đức being doused with gasoline outside the Cambodian Embassy in Saigon on 11 June 1963. Shortly afterwards, he set himself on fire as a protest against Diem's rule. US reporters had been tipped off to encourage their presence.

1 Give **two** things you can infer from Source A about Diem's rule in South Vietnam. **(4)**

Complete the table below to explain your answer.

(i) What I can infer:

Details in the source that tell me this:

(ii) What I can infer:

Details in the source that tell me this:

2 Explain why the USA was concerned about the future of Vietnam in 1963. **(12)**

You **may** use the following in your answer:

- the division of the country into North and South
- Diem's government

You **must** also use information of your own.

EXAM TIP 

When answering question 2, remember P-E-E:

- Make your **P**oint.
- Back it up with **E**vidence from your historical knowledge.
- Then **E**xplain why your chosen point caused the result in the question.

Do this three times and you'll have your answer! You can add an introductory paragraph if you wish, but there is no need to add a conclusion.

Knowledge

8 The escalation of the conflict in Vietnam under Johnson

The increasing threat of the Vietcong

The removal of Diem failed to stop support for the Vietcong growing.

- In November 1963, President Kennedy was assassinated. Vice President Lyndon Johnson replaced him, then won the 1964 presidential election.
- The Vietcong were increasingly successful in expanding their influence in South Vietnam through both **propaganda** and presence.

Propaganda	Presence
• The Vietcong spread propaganda amongst the population. • Its members claimed to fight to end poverty and injustice, and to unite Vietnam. • They lived with villagers, introduced social reforms, and showed the people respect.	• By the end of 1964, around two-thirds of South Vietnam was under Vietcong control. • The Vietcong had around 100 000 soldiers, but also much more civilian support. • Vietcong bases were established in jungles throughout the South. • The Vietcong operated amongst, and blended into, the local population. • Supply routes brought weapons from China and the USSR overland along the Ho Chi Minh trail through Laos and Cambodia (see page 28), and by sea. • Between 1955 and 1963, China sent North Vietnam over $100 million in aid.
• Members of the ARVN were portrayed as weak and puppets of the USA. • South Vietnamese villagers resented being relocated into hamlets.	• The ARVN and US troops totalled around 550 000 soldiers by the end of 1964. • The South Vietnamese government was divided by in-fighting after Diem's removal, and was not fully focused on fighting the war. • The USA's presence was increasingly unpopular in South Vietnam and was linked to the failing regime.

The Gulf of Tonkin incident, 1964

Johnson wanted to increase efforts to contain communism in Vietnam. An attack on a US ship in the Gulf of Tonkin gave him the chance:

- USS *Maddox* was attacked by North Vietnamese torpedo boats on 2 August 1964.
- Further follow-up attacks on *Maddox* and USS *Turner Joy* were claimed on 4 August, but have since been disproved.

These 'attacks' were followed by US aircraft bombing North Vietnam.

- Johnson had warned against more 'unprovoked' attacks'. He now asked Congress to pass a resolution for military action and for political and financial support against aggression.
- Congress agreed, with only two votes against.

President Johnson signed the Tonkin Resolution (10 August 1964):

- It gave Johnson power to 'take all necessary measures to repel any armed attack against the forces of the United States and to prevent further aggression'
- It pushed North Vietnam into further aiding the Vietcong.

The nature of the conflict in Vietnam, 1964–68

- US tactics were designed to exploit the USA's aerial superiority and destroy North Vietnam's ability to wage war.
- However, the Vietcong did not fight a conventional war, and proved a challenging opponent. The Vietcong used guerrilla tactics to great effect.

Guerrilla tactic	Why it was effective
No uniforms	This meant members of the Vietcong were hard to identify. They were indistinguishable from peasants, and soldiers were afraid of killing innocent people.
Peasants	Vietcong guerrillas gained support by being very respectful and never stealing from peasants.
Punishing traitors	The Vietcong were generous to those who helped them but brutal to those who helped the enemy. Some 30 000 collaborators were executed during the war.
Tunnels	Complex tunnel systems that had been used against the French and Japanese were expanded. The tunnels offered protection against bombing, storage, and shelter, and were hard to find and target with counter-attacks.
Booby traps	Ingenious and vicious traps such as punji stick pits, grenade traps, snake pits, bamboo whips, and mines were a danger to US soldiers. During the Vietnam War, 11% of US deaths and 15% of injuries were caused by booby traps.
Ambushes	The Vietcong launched hit-and-run surprise attacks, before melting away into the jungle, keeping their enemy in constant fear of attack. They also sabotaged roads and bridges to interrupt transport links, and targeted military equipment.
Ho Chi Minh Trail	This ensured Vietcong bases in the South could be resupplied. As the trail went through neighbouring Laos and Cambodia, the USA could not attack it directly.

From November 1964, the Vietcong in the South received greater support from the North. Those fighting for the Vietcong were urged to attack US bases, not just the ARVN.

The Vietcong's guerrilla tactics brought successes with minimal casualties.

December 1964/January 1965:

Vietcong victory at Binh Gia:

- some 50 US helicopters destroyed
- around 200 US/ARVN troops killed
- the death of only 32 Vietcong soldiers.

7 February 1965:

Vietcong raid Pleiku airfield in a five-minute attack:

- over 120 US/ARVN casualties
- at least 20 aircraft damaged
- the death of only one Vietcong soldier.

Why did the Vietcong use guerrilla tactics?

- Ho Chi Minh had fought guerrilla wars against both the French and Japanese.
- They suited smaller numbers of less-equipped troops, who could be more mobile and disguise themselves as peasants to hide in plain sight and disappear after fighting.
- Using the cover of the jungle, setting traps, and sabotaging US equipment and supplies frustrated the US military and damaged the ARVN's **morale**.
- The longer the war went on and the more US casualties increased, the more unpopular and unwinnable the war would seem to the US public.

Knowledge

8 The escalation of the conflict in Vietnam under Johnson

Methods used by the USA

By February 1965, US involvement in Vietnam was costing $2 million a day. Over 180 000 US troops had been sent to Vietnam, and almost 2000 had been killed in action.

The USA used three main methods of fighting the Vietcong. These tactics were destructive and caused a lot of **collateral damage**, increasing local resentment.

1 Search and Destroy

From March 1965: Increasing numbers of US ground troops were sent to Vietnam. They used 'search and destroy' tactics.

- US troops entered villages searching for Vietcong camps and supplies. If evidence was found, the villages were destroyed by fire or bombing.
- Some missions succeeded, but they made US troops susceptible to booby traps, and alienated locals.
- As soon as the US troops left, the Vietcong moved back in; around three million South Vietnamese were made homeless.
- Johnson had to use the **draft** to forcibly recruit soldiers, causing resentment in the USA.

2 Operation Rolling Thunder

From 2 March 1965 to 2 November 1968: A **strategic** bombing campaign called Operation Rolling Thunder was waged against military and industrial areas in North Vietnam and the Ho Chi Minh Trail.

- Johnson initially set the target areas, but the scope widened as resistance continued.
- 643 000 tonnes of bombs were dropped over 3.5 years.
- It cost $900 million but only caused around $300 million in damage; 900 US aircraft were shot down.
- It led to 52 000 casualties, over 34 000 of whom were civilians. This made the USA look barbaric and only served to strengthen Ho Chi Minh's resolve.
- It failed to stop use of the Trail, as it was constantly repaired, and the tunnels protected soldiers/supplies.
- It failed to disrupt war supplies, as most came from China and the USSR, countries the USA did not want to risk conflict with.

3 Chemical weapons

From 1962 to 1971: Operation Ranch Hand oversaw the aerial spraying of **defoliants** over South Vietnam.

- Powerful herbicides were used to clear jungle plants and crops.
- Some 3000 villages over 4.5 million acres were sprayed, often with the villagers still in residence.
- Agent Orange was used to destroy the jungle and expose Vietcong bases and supply routes.
- Agent Blue was used to kill crops.
- The defoliants damaged soil and harmed people for decades, with high incidences of skin disease, miscarriage, cancer, birth defects, and malformations reported.
- **Napalm**, an **incendiary** designed to burn anything on contact, was also used extensively. Its use against civilians was banned in 1980.

Increased US involvement in Vietnam

The late 1960s saw increased US involvement in the war in Vietnam, and a corresponding increase in spending:

	1964	1965	1968
Number of US troops sent to Vietnam	23 000	184 000	536 000
Number of US troops killed in the war	206	1863	16 592
US cost of the Vietnam War	$500 million	$700 million	$26 266 million

The Tet Offensive, 1968

There were few large-scale battles in the Vietnam War. The biggest – and most significant – was the Tet Offensive of January and February 1968.

The Tet Lunar New Year was one of Vietnam's biggest holidays, and a ceasefire usually took place during the festival. The Vietcong attack took US and ARVN forces by surprise.

Late 1967: Areas near the border are attacked to lure the US and ARVN troops north.

21 Jan 1968: North Vietnamese troops attack the US base at Khe Sanh. The USA sends 6000 troops to defend the base.

30 Jan 1968: The Vietcong attack 13 cities in South Vietnam. Most ARVN troops are not on duty because of the holiday.

31 Jan 1968: North Vietnamese and Vietcong forces strike more than 120 cities, towns, and military bases throughout South Vietnam.

19 Vietcong attack the US embassy in the capital, Saigon. Although 18 are killed, they briefly hold the bottom floor of the embassy.

24 Feb 1968: Vietcong troops are forced out of Hue. US and ARVN forces find evidence of a massacre. Over 500 US marines and ARVN are killed reclaiming Hue's ancient citadel, filmed by numerous TV crews.

27 Feb 1968: The leading TV news reporter in the USA, Walter Cronkite, suggests in a report that the war is unwinnable. President Johnson allegedly responds: 'If I've lost Cronkite, I've lost middle America.'

Although initially very successful, the communist forces were spread thin, and US and ARVN forces countered most of the attacks successfully.

Significance of the Tet Offensive

By 1968, public opinion in the USA was turning against the war in Vietnam. The Tet Offensive was a crucial factor, resulting in almost 13 000 US and ARVN casualties. The US media and public believed the war could not be won, despite heavy Vietcong losses.

Impact of the Tet Offensive		
...on the Vietcong	**...on South Vietnam**	**...on the USA**
• The USA estimated 60 000 communist troops were killed (a figure since revised down). It was a significant blow to the Vietcong's military capacity. • The Vietcong gained no new ground in South Vietnam. • The offensive failed to provoke an uprising of support among the peasants in South Vietnam.	• The ARVN proved they could be an effective fighting force. • The offensive showed the ARVN had some support, as there was no uprising against them. • The offensive highlighted the destruction of a communist takeover: almost 8000 civilians died, and 75 000 homes were destroyed.	• The invasion of the US embassy shocked many Americans, who thought the USA was winning. • US General Westmoreland requested a further 200 000 troops to launch a counteroffensive, but only 10 500 were sent. • US public opinion became more strongly anti-war. Protests in the USA increased, as the end of the war was not in sight. • By late 1968, Westmoreland and Johnson had left their roles. Johnson announced he would not stand for President again.

Key terms Make sure you can write a definition for these key terms

propaganda morale collateral damage draft strategic defoliant napalm incendiary

Retrieval

Learn the answers to the questions below, then cover the answers column with a piece of paper and write down as many as you can. Check and repeat until you know them all.

	Questions	Answers
1	Which event in 1964 involved attacks on the American naval destroyer USS *Maddox*?	The Gulf of Tonkin incident
2	What happened after the attacks in the Gulf of Tonkin?	Congress agreed to give Johnson the authority to escalate the war in Vietnam
3	What was the Ho Chi Minh Trail?	A route from North to South Vietnam used to resupply guerrilla groups in the South
4	Name the way of fighting used by the small groups of Vietcong.	Guerrilla warfare
5	How did the Vietcong treat South Vietnamese people working with the USA?	The Vietcong were brutal to those seen as traitors; around 30 000 collaborators were executed
6	What was 'search and destroy'?	A US military tactic that involved US troops entering villages hunting Vietcong; if evidence of Vietcong was found, the villages were destroyed
7	What was Operation Rolling Thunder?	A US strategic bombing campaign that dropped 643 000 tonnes of bombs on North Vietnam and the Ho Chi Minh Trail
8	Name two controversial chemical weapons used by the USA?	Two from: Agent Orange / Agent Blue / napalm
9	By how much did Johnson increase the US military presence in Vietnam in the four years after Tonkin?	In 1964 there were 23 000 US troops in Vietnam; by 1968 there were 536 000 US troops – an increase of 513 000
10	Why was the Tet Offensive a surprise for the ARVN and US troops?	In previous years, there had been a ceasefire during the Tet holiday, which was the lunar new year
11	Why was the Tet Offensive a success for the Vietcong?	The US media and public believed the war could not be won, despite heavy Vietcong losses

Put paper here

Previous questions

Use the questions below to check your knowledge from previous chapters.

	Questions	Answers
1	What did the Supreme Court fail to do in *Brown* v. *Topeka*, and what was the long-term effect?	It failed to give a deadline for integration, so progress was slow as states delayed or resisted
2	Why was the 1968 Mexico Olympics significant for the idea of 'Black Power'?	Two Black athletes gave the Black Power salute when receiving their medals, gaining widespread media attention for the cause
3	How did Kennedy escalate the US presence in Vietnam?	He increased support for Diem's regime from 700 military advisers to 16 000 and increased funding

Put paper here

Practice 8

Exam-style questions

Study Sources A and B.

1 How useful are Sources A and B for an enquiry into the bombing campaigns during the Vietnam War? Explain your answer, using Sources A and B and your knowledge of the historical context. **(8)**

Source A: An extract from the book *Mission with LeMay: My Story*, published in 1965. LeMay was head of the US Air Force in 1965.

Apply whatever force it is necessary to employ, to stop things quickly. The main thing is stop it. The quicker you stop it, the more lives you save. My solution to the problem would be to tell [the North Vietnamese Communists] frankly that they've got to stop their aggression or we're going to bomb them into the Stone Age. And we would shove them back into the Stone Age with Air power or Naval power—not with ground forces.

Source B: An extract from a December 1998 interview with Robert McNamara, United States Secretary of Defense from 1961 to 1968.

No more military pressure could have been applied … We dropped two or three times as many bombs in North and South Vietnam as were dropped by all Allied Forces throughout World War II against all enemies. It was a tremendous air effort. But there are certain things bombing can't accomplish. They can't break the will of people. They didn't break the will of the North Vietnamese. And it cannot stop the movement of the small quantities of supplies that were necessary to support the Vietcong and the North Vietnamese forces in the South.

Study Interpretations 1 and 2. They give different views about the bombing campaigns during the Vietnam War.

2 What is the main difference between these views? Explain your answer, using details from both interpretations **(4)**

Interpretation 1: Adapted from 'Was Operation Rolling Thunder a Failure?' on the US History Channel's website.

Although North Vietnam did not have much of an air force, its leaders managed to mount an effective defense using surface-to-air missiles and radar-controlled anti-aircraft artillery from China and the Soviet Union. They shot down hundreds of American planes, constructed networks of bombproof tunnels and shelters, and dispatched crews by night to rebuild damage. Additionally, the communists used the destructive air strikes for propaganda purposes to increase anti-American sentiment and patriotism among North Vietnamese citizens.

Interpretation 2: Adapted from Global Security, an independent military history and news website. It discusses the flaws of Operation Rolling Thunder.

Rolling Thunder failed to intimidate the North Vietnamese and it failed to destroy their ability to fight. It had no clear-cut objective nor did its authors have any real estimate of the cost of lives and aircraft. The failure of the American military to develop a plan consistent with the limits of war fought for limited objectives caused a crippling clash of plan and perceptions. As a result, air power was unwillingly tasked to perform a mission for which it was ill-equipped and unprepared.

3 Suggest **one** reason why Interpretations 1 and 2 give different views about the bombing campaigns during the Vietnam War. You may use Sources A and B to help explain your answer. **(4)**

4 How far do you agree with Interpretation 1 about the bombing campaigns during the Vietnam War? Explain your answer, using both interpretations and your knowledge of the historical context. **(16)**

EXAM TIP

Question 4 is worth 16 marks, but there is an additional 4 marks available for spelling, punctuation and grammar. Be sure to leave time to read through your answer and check your writing.

9 Changes under Nixon, 1969–73

The Nixon Doctrine

- By August 1968, Johnson's approval ratings were down to 36%. His public appearances were met by protesters chanting 'Hey, hey, LBJ, how many kids did you kill today?'
- In the 1968 election campaign, Richard Nixon promised a plan to resolve the conflict in Vietnam.
- Nixon went on to win the 1968 presidential election with a clear majority, Johnson having withdrawn his candidacy early in the campaign due to a lack of popular support.

▲ *President Richard Nixon*

Election tactics	Presidential actions	
Nixon promised 'peace with honour' in Vietnam.	Nixon initiated secret talks with North Vietnam without involving or telling South Vietnam.	The USA secretly bombed the Ho Chi Minh Trail in Cambodia in March 1969.
Nixon promised to end the draft into the army.	US forces in Vietnam focused on training the ARVN.	Nixon introduced the policy of 'Vietnamisation': the USA promised military and financial aid to the ARVN whilst withdrawing US troops.
Nixon encouraged the Vietcong representative at the Paris peace talks to delay talks until after the election.	Nixon put forward the 'Nixon **Doctrine**' on 25 July 1969, promising US allies in Asia support, including nuclear support, but no troops.	

Vietnamisation

'**Vietnamisation**' was Nixon's plan to withdraw US troops without losing the war.

Although Vietnamisation reduced the US military presence in Vietnam, some feared the withdrawal was too soon for the ARVN; others felt it was not quick enough for the US troops.

Weaknesses of Vietnamisation	Strengths of Vietnamisation
The ARVN was badly led, had low morale, and was weakened by corruption and incompetence. Attempts to use US air power to shut down the Ho Chi Minh Trail failed. The remaining US troops had very low morale, drug use was high, and **fragging** increased (more than 300 cases, 1969–70).	60 000 US troops were withdrawn from Vietnam by late 1969. By 1971, fewer than 200 000 remained. The withdrawal was popular with the US public. The ARVN grew from 820 000 in 1968 to over one million by 1971. US casualties dropped significantly: from 11 600 in 1969, to 6000 in 1970, and just over 2000 in 1971.

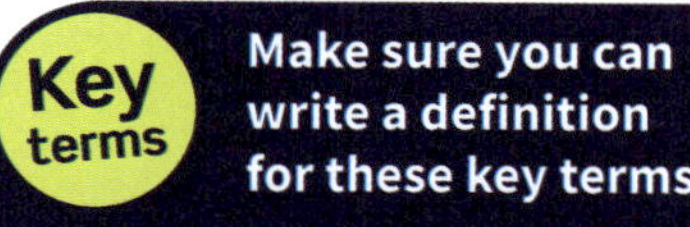

doctrine Vietnamisation fragging

Attacks on Cambodia (1970) and Laos (1971)

In 1970 and 1971, Nixon expanded the war into neighbouring Cambodia and Laos (see map on page 28) to cut the Ho Chi Minh Trail and stop the spread of communism.

Cambodia

- Cambodia was neutral in the Vietnam War until a pro-US general took over and demanded that the North Vietnamese leave in March 1970.
- In April 1970, around 80 000 ARVN and US troops invaded in support of the new government.
- Attacks were restricted to within 30 miles of the Vietnamese border.
- Around 11 000 communists were killed.
- Shocked, Congress revoked the Gulf of Tonkin Resolution in June.

Verdict: Failure

✗ Supply lines were not badly affected, as the Vietcong could use Laos instead.
✗ US public outrage increased.
✗ Anti-war protests in the USA intensified.

Laos

- Laos was also neutral in the war, with several groups fighting for power, some communist.
- In February 1971, the USA provided air support for an ARVN invasion of over 20 000 troops to sever the Ho Chi Minh Trail.
- 36 000 North Vietnamese counterattacked in March and drove the ARVN out of the country, causing heavy casualties.

Verdict: Failure

✗ Supply lines remained secure.
✗ North Vietnam's success led it to launch the Easter Offensive into South Vietnam with 120 000 troops in 1972.

The bombing of North Vietnam (1972)

In response to the Easter Offensive, Nixon launched Operation Linebacker on 6 April 1972. This was a bombing campaign to force North Vietnam to negotiate for peace. It lasted into October of that year.

Operation Linebacker was followed by a second operation – Linebacker II – in December 1972, which lasted 12 days, and killed over 1600 civilians.

- No restrictions: the key cities of Hanoi and Haiphong were bombed.
- Mines were dropped in Haiphong harbour and a naval blockade kept Chinese and Soviet ships away.
- The bombing nearly destroyed North Vietnam's war industry and severely disrupted supplies.

Verdict: Success

✓ On 26 December, urged on by its allies, North Vietnam agreed to resume peace negotiations with the USA.

Reasons for the failure of Vietnamisation

Vietnamisation failed for three main reasons:

South Vietnam	The economy suffered: 300 000 South Vietnamese lost their jobs as they were reliant on US troops. The government was weak, divided, and unpopular.
The ARVN	There was low morale and little will to fight; desertion was common. Training had been hurried; officers had limited experience. Corruption led to unsuitable appointments and supplies being sold off.
US troops	Troops knew the end was coming, so there was no incentive to risk their lives fighting.

Retrieval

Learn the answers to the questions below, then cover the answers column with a piece of paper and write down as many as you can. Check and repeat until you know them all.

	Questions	Answers
1	How was President Johnson's popularity affected by the Vietnam War?	His popularity dropped from 77% to to 36%; people chanted 'Hey, hey, LBJ, how many kids did you kill today?'
2	What did Nixon promise to end (other than the war) to gain popular support?	The draft
3	What was the 'Nixon Doctrine'?	Nixon's plan, put forward in July 1969, promising US allies in Asia support, including nuclear support, but no US troops would be involved
4	What was Vietnamisation?	Nixon's promise to provide military and financial support to the ARVN but to withdraw US troops
5	How many US troops were withdrawn from Vietnam by late 1969?	60 000
6	What happened to the ARVN as a result of Vietnamisation?	It grew to over one million by 1971; however, the ARVN was badly led, had low morale, and was affected by corruption and incompetence
7	What happened to US casualties in Vietnam in the years after Vietnamisation began?	They dropped significantly, from 11 600 in 1969 to just over 2000 in 1971
8	How did Vietnamisation affect US troops?	The remaining US troops had very low morale, drug use was common, and fragging increased
9	Which two countries did Nixon extend the war into, and when?	Cambodia (April 1970) and Laos (February 1971)
10	What effect did events in Cambodia have in the USA?	Congress was shocked and revoked the Gulf of Tonkin Resolution; protest in the USA intensified
11	How did events in December 1972 change the course of the war?	12 days of US bombing encouraged North Vietnam to agree to resume peace negotiations

Put paper here

Previous questions

Use the questions below to check your knowledge from previous chapters.

	Questions	Answers
1	Why was the Till case unique in Mississippi history?	It was the first time white men had been tried for the murder of a Black man
2	How comparable were the poverty rates for Black and white Americans by 1975?	Black Americans were three times more likely to live in poverty
3	By how much did Johnson increase the US military presence in Vietnam in the four years after Tonkin?	In 1964 there were 23 000 US troops in Vietnam; by 1968 there were 536 000 US troops – an increase of 513 000

Put paper here

Practice

Exam-style questions

Study Source A below and then answer Question 1.

Source A: The motorcade of President Lyndon Johnson is attacked by anti-Vietnam War protesters in Melbourne, Australia. Protesters threw paint on the car, police, and Secret Service agents on 21 October 1966.

SOURCE TIP

Writing out a quotation or describing what is shown in an image does not show an inference. You need to extract information not explicit in the source. For example, what does the fact that the president's car is covered in paint suggest about the feelings of the surrounding crowd? What does the location of the photo suggest?

1 Give **two** things you can infer from Source A about President Johnson's approach to the Vietnam War. **(4)**

Complete the table below to explain your answer.

(i) What I can infer:
Details in the source that tell me this:
(ii) What I can infer:
Details in the source that tell me this:

2 Explain why Nixon took a different approach to the Vietnam War to Johnson. **(12)**

You **may** use the following in your answer:

- anti-war protest in the USA
- the ARVN

You **must** also use information of your own.

EXAM TIP

The prompts given here refer to two reasons why Nixon took a different approach to Johnson. Remember to use the prompts to explain why: for example, Johnson's increasing unpopularity (see Source A) and the benefits to the USA of training the ARVN.

Knowledge

10 Opposition to, and support for, the Vietnam War

Opposition to the war

Most people in the USA had no opinion on Vietnam during the Eisenhower (1953–61) and Kennedy (1961–63) years.

Johnson's decision to deploy ground troops from March 1965 led to a growing anti-war movement. Around 70% of the US public supported the war in 1965, and around 68% opposed it by 1971; both figures give the highest percentages of support for or against the war.

Reasons for the growth of opposition to the war:

- The Vietnam War was the first conflict broadcast widely on national TV. There was unprecedented, uncensored media coverage of the conflict.
- People felt the war was unfair (the USA was powerful and wealthy), unjustified, and carried the risk of becoming nuclear.
- Many young American men feared conscription from the draft. There was also a belief that the draft targeted the poor whilst the rich escaped ('draft dodging').
- Key national figures opposed the war, including Martin Luther King, Muhammad Ali, and John Lennon.
- The costs of the war kept growing, both in terms of American lives lost and money – resulting in a tax increase in 1968.
- A growing student counter-culture movement, including the SDS (Students for a Democratic Society), rejected their parents' values and called for social change.
- There was a growing interest in Eastern spiritualism through the hippy movement, which was anti-war and challenged traditional values.
- In 1967, 'Vietnam Veterans Against the War' formed to protest against the war. They handed in medals received during the war and gathered evidence of atrocities committed.

The My Lai Massacre, 1968

Disastrous operations such as C Company's 'search and destroy' mission at the village of My Lai in March 1968 provided further fuel for anti-war protesters.

- US soldiers murdered around 500 civilians.
- The US military reported that they had successfully destroyed a Vietcong base.
- War photographer Sergeant Haeberle took pictures that helped expose the truth.
- The military cover-up was exposed and the lieutenant in charge put on trial. He was sentenced to life imprisonment, but his superiors were not charged.
- Lieutenant Calley was released by President Nixon after only serving three years.

The massacre and cover-up:

- increased public opposition to the war
- increased distrust of the US government
- harmed US soldiers' morale
- caused international condemnation.

However, My Lai was not a unique incident.

The Kent State shootings, 1970

Following the US invasion of Cambodia, around 500 students launched an anti-war protest at Kent State University, Ohio, on 1 May 1970. The protests escalated into violence and tragedy.

- As the number of protesters grew to 1000, fighting broke out between anti-war protesters and pro-war demonstrators.
- On 2 May, the Campus Officer Training Corps building was burnt down.
- The Mayor of Ohio declared a state of emergency and sent in troopers.
- On 4 May, around 3000 protestors held demonstration. When troopers ordered the protesters to leave, they refused and threw rocks.
- The state troopers retaliated, firing tear gas into the crowd, which threw more rocks. The troopers opened fire on the crowd, killing four students and injuring nine.

The shooting of white, middle-class students on a university campus horrified middle-class Americans and resulted in a storm of media attention.

Support for the war

People supported the Vietnam War for a variety of reasons, although support declined over time. Nevertheless, substantial numbers still supported military action after 1968, including some students.

US politicians were equally split between anti-war 'Doves' and pro-war 'Hawks'.

Reason for supporting the war	Explanation	Example
Fear of communism	Domino theory was a powerful influence on US public opinion. When China became communist, every country in Asia seemed at risk.	The **Red Scare** of 1950–53 was a 'witch hunt' of supposed communists in the USA.
Media support	Until 1968, most of the 600 US journalists in Vietnam were based in the relative safety of Saigon, and got their stories from the Joint US Public Affairs Office.	Walter Cronkite supported the war upto 1968; he was critical in turning US public opinion after that.
Patriotism	Many Americans were highly patriotic. They believed in the overwhelming power of the US Army and were certain that it was on the side of good, fighting for freedom and democracy. Challenging this was seen as treasonous.	Involvement in the Second World War and the defeat of the Nazis cemented the USA's place in world affairs. Americans did not want to 'lose face' in Vietnam.
'Hard hats'	Working-class white men, sometimes known as 'hard hats' (referring to hard hats worn in the construction industry), had often served in the US military and had sons who were fighting. Their support was unwavering.	In the 'hard hat' riot of 1970, 200 New York construction workers pushed through police to attack people protesting against the Kent State shootings.
The **'silent majority'**	A large group of conservative, traditional Americans believed in the values of the USA and the government's duty to preserve them and spread them globally, but did not protest either for or against the war. They backed Nixon's call for an 'honorable peace'.	Nixon appealed to the 'great silent majority' in a speech in November 1969. A later poll showed that 77% supported his policies in Vietnam.
Peace negotiations	These began in 1968 in Paris. Occasional ceasefires and walk-outs occurred, but there was hope among the US public that the negotiations could end the conflict.	'Peace with Honor' was Nixon's description of the 1973 peace deal.
Political support	Political support was complicated by party politics, popular opinion, and desire for the USA not to appear defeated. The government was not always transparent or honest about the cost of its commitments, and the military continued to claim that victory was near.	After 1970, Congress began restricting the funds available for the war, but continued to make money available. US politicians feared a communist South Vietnam.

After Nixon's 'silent majority' speech, polls showed that many US citizens considered themselves part of that group. Both the House of Representatives and the Senate passed resolutions supporting Nixon's war policies.

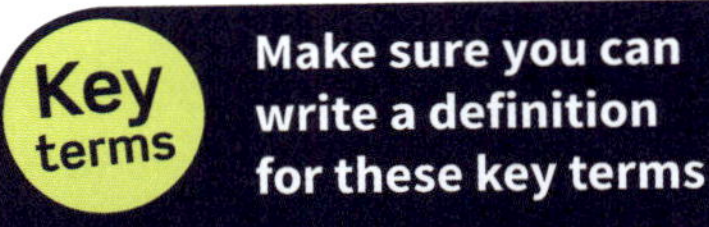

Red Scare   patriotism   'hard hats'   'silent majority'

Retrieval

Learn the answers to the questions below, then cover the answers column with a piece of paper and write down as many as you can. Check and repeat until you know them all.

	Questions	Answers
1	What year saw the highest percentage of people supporting the war in Vietnam?	1965; around 70% of the population were in support of the war
2	What year saw the highest percentage of people opposing the war in Vietnam?	1971; around 68% of the population were in opposition to the war
3	How did US media coverage of the Vietnam War increase opposition to it?	The Vietnam War was the first conflict broadcast widely on national TV. There was unprecedented, uncensored media coverage of the conflict.
4	Which group felt most affected by the draft?	Poor, young men
5	In what year did Congress approve a tax increase to pay for the Vietnam War?	1968
6	What happened at My Lai in 1968 that increased opposition to the war?	Over 500 unarmed Vietnamese civilians were killed by US soldiers; the massacre was covered up
7	What happened at Kent State University in 1970 that increased opposition to the war?	Four students were shot dead by state troopers during a protest against the Cambodia invasion
8	What was the biggest fear of those who supported the war?	That defeat might lead to a domino effect, which would mean an increase in communist countries
9	Who were the 'hard hats'?	Working-class men who supported the Vietnam War; many had served in the armed forces
10	What phrase did Nixon use to describe the large numbers of US citizens who supported the war but were ignored by the media?	The 'silent majority'
11	What percentage of Americans supported Nixon's war policies after his famous speech in November 1969?	77%

Put paper here

Previous questions

Use the questions below to check your knowledge from previous chapters.

	Questions	Answers
1	How many children were arrested during the Birmingham campaign?	Over 900
2	What happened to Diem in November 1963?	He was removed by his own generals in a coup encouraged by the CIA, arrested, and shot dead
3	What was Vietnamisation?	Nixon's promise to provide military and financial support to the ARVN but to withdraw US troops

Put paper here

Exam-style questions

Study Sources A and B.

1 How useful are Sources A and B for an enquiry into opposition to the Vietnam War? Explain your answer, using Sources A and B and your knowledge of the historical context. **(8)**

Source A: An extract from an interview with Peter J. Brennan, president of the Building and Construction Trades Council of Greater New York, following the 'hard hat' riot of 1970.

Telephone calls and letters received by the unions were 20 to 1 in favor of the construction workers who were involved in a confrontation with antiwar demonstrators here last Friday. The demonstration was spontaneous. The unions had nothing to do with it, the men acted on their own. They did it because they were fed up with violence by anti-war demonstrators, by those who spat at the American flag and desecrated it. We've had calls and letters from all over the country praising the workers for their patriotism.

Source B: An extract from a speech entitled 'We ain't goin' delivered by Stokely Carmichael, leader of the SNCC, on 4 November 1967. (This source uses a racist term for Black people which was deeply offensive at the time and is considered to be unacceptable today.)

*You ought to recognize what's going on in that Vietnamese War. Here they taking you, training you to be a soldier, making you shine your shoes until three o'clock in the morning, going 8000 miles to shoot a man and he ain't never called you a n*****. Yeah.*

Now we are not only opposed [to] the war in Vietnam, we're opposed to compulsory conscription. We are against the draft. Now we're against the draft for anybody – Black or white.

Study Interpretations 1 and 2. They give different views about opposition to the Vietnam War.

2 What is the main difference between these views? Explain your answer, using details from both interpretations. **(4)**

Interpretation 1: Adapted from *A People's History of the United States*, written by historian Howard Zinn in 1980.

The publicity given to the student protests created the impression that the opposition to the war came mostly from middle-class intellectuals. When some construction workers in New York attacked student demonstrators, the news was played up in the national media. However, a number of elections in American cities, including those where mostly blue-collar workers lived, showed that anti-war sentiment was strong in the working classes. For instance, in Dearborn, Michigan, an automobile manufacturing town, a poll as early as 1967 showed 41% of the population favored withdrawal from the Vietnam war.

Interpretation 2: Adapted from *A History of the United States*, written by historian Philip Jenkins in 1997.

Anti-war protest found an enthusiastic home in college campuses, and campus demonstrations and sit-ins became commonplace in the spring of 1968. Violent conflicts with police became even more frequent, as did active draft resistance and the destruction of draft cards. For conservatives, the protesters were literally committing treason against the nation and its soldiers, who were facing death on the battlefields of South East Asia. Anti-war militants even carried the Vietcong flag in demonstrations, deliberately seeking to enrage conservatives.

3 Suggest **one** reason why Interpretations 1 and 2 give different views about opposition to the Vietnam War. **(4)**

4 How far do you agree with Interpretation 1 about opposition to the Vietnam War? Explain your answer, using both interpretations and your knowledge of the historical context. **(16)**

EXAM TIP

Question 3 invites you to also refer to the two sources from question 1 in your answer. This may help you to demonstrate different reasons why the interpretations differ.

Knowledge

11 The peace process and the end of the Vietnam War

Reasons for and features of the peace negotiations, 1965–73

There were various reasons why the USA decided to negotiate for peace in Vietnam. These included the consequences of the Tet Offensive, the problems of pursuing the conflict at home and in Vietnam, and a desire for peace.

April 1965
US President Johnson states his willingness to talk, but only if an independent South Vietnam is agreed.
North Vietnam offers to discuss a united Vietnam, as agreed in the Geneva Accords, along with the withdrawal of US troops.

May 1968
The North demands a halt to US bombing; the USA seeks a reduction of Vietcong activities in the South. However, whilst both sides see a need to talk, the post-Tet Offensive Paris peace talks stall, because neither side budges.

November 1968
Johnson halts all US bombing to try to restart peace talks.

January 1969
Peace talks resume after Nixon becomes President, having promised to swiftly end the war. Nixon begins talks with China and the USSR as part of negotiations aimed at reducing conflict in the Cold War.

February 1970
Nixon's foreign policy adviser, Henry Kissinger, begins secret talks with North Vietnam.

1969–71
Ongoing negotiations fail to produce a significant breakthrough.
Vietnamisation reduces US troop numbers to 25 000 by 1972.
Congress starts restricting the level of funds available to prosecute the war.

February 1972
Nixon visits China, the first US President to do so since China became communist in 1949. He hopes to persuade the Chinese to reduce support for North Vietnam.

March 1972
The Vietcong Easter Offensive exposes the weakness of the ARVN without US troops, but fails to achieve its target. It becomes clear the war could drag on indefinitely.

Apr–Dec 1972
Operations Linebacker and Linebacker II maintain large-scale bombing of North Vietnamese positions.

May 1972
Nixon visits the USSR, the first US President to do so since the USSR became communist in 1917. His aim is to negotiate nuclear arms reduction and reduce Soviet support for North Vietnam.

October 1972
After the failure of the Easter Offensive and the success of US efforts with China and the USSR, North Vietnam finally agrees to recognise the government of South Vietnam, provided a peace deal includes processes for free elections and political reform. South Vietnam refuses, breaking up the talks.

December 1972
Operation Linebacker II, and pressure from China and the USSR, bring North Vietnam back to the talks.

January 1973
The Paris Peace Accords are signed, ending the Vietnam War.

The significance of the Paris Peace Accords, 1973

The Paris Peace Accords allowed the USA to withdraw from Vietnam without admitting defeat, but in Vietnam itself it was never more than a pause in the conflict.

Terms of the Paris Peace Accords	What happened
✓ Withdrawal of all US and allied forces within 60 days.	US troops were withdrawn.
✓ Ceasefire in South Vietnam following the divisions of the 1954 Geneva Agreements.	The ceasefire lasted only until December 1974, when North Vietnam invaded the South. The capital of South Vietnam, Saigon, finally fell in April 1975.
✓ Reunification of Vietnam through peaceful means without invasion by either country, and without foreign interference.	The collapse of the South's economy after the US withdrawal meant that the communists were mostly welcomed. Vietnam was united on 2 July 1976 to form the communist Socialist Republic of Vietnam.
✓ Withdrawal of foreign troops from Laos and Cambodia.	US troops were withdrawn, but Vietnam invaded Cambodia in 1978.
✓ Financial contributions from the USA to 'heal the wounds of war' throughout Indochina.	A figure of $3.25 billion was discussed, but no money was ever received, partly because of the failure of both sides to uphold other parts of the peace agreement.

The economic and human costs of the war for the USA

Human costs

- More than one in every 100 Americans served in Vietnam.
- The cost of the war was high, especially amongst those that survived the fighting.
- Many struggled with drug addiction, unemployment, marriage break-ups, and even suicide.

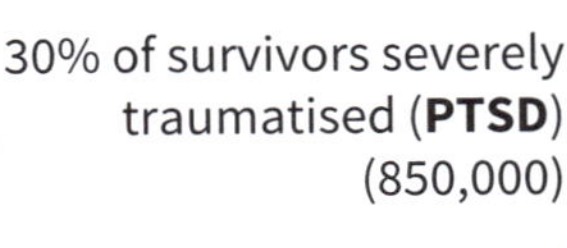

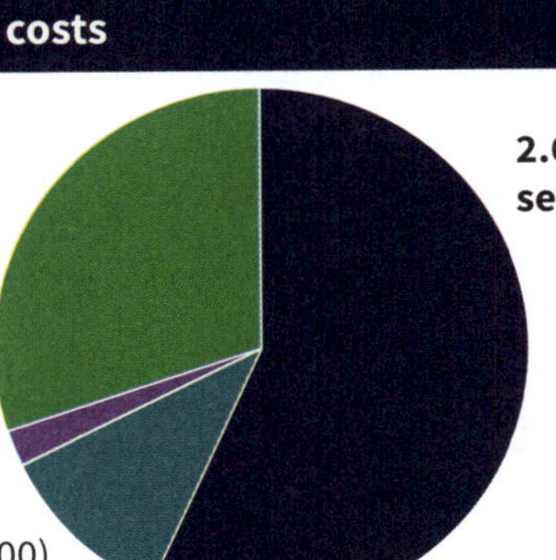

Economic costs

- The economic cost of the war was $168 billion, or $1 trillion in today's money. This included $111 billion in military operations and $28.5 billion in aid to South Vietnam.
- Martin Luther King once estimated that the war cost $322 000 per enemy dead, whilst the US government only spent about $53 per person supporting each poor American.

Costs to US government

- The Vietnam War saw a significant erosion of public faith in the US government.
- Johnson's approval ratings dropped from 77% when he won the presidency in 1964 to 36% by 1974.

Knowledge

11 The peace process and the end of the Vietnam War

Reasons for the failure of the USA in Vietnam

North Vietnamese strengths

The USA lost face abroad over Vietnam. By 1975, the whole of Vietnam was communist, whilst the USA was a divided nation. But why did the USA – a global superpower – lose?

The US defeat was the result of both North Vietnamese strengths and US weaknesses.

North Vietnamese strengths	
The Ho Chi Minh Trail allowed guerrilla groups in the South to be resupplied throughout the war. The USA could not destroy the trail because it went through Laos and Cambodia.	✓
The USSR and China supported North Vietnam with money, military aid, and, in the case of China, over 300 000 troops. The aid often included sophisticated modern weaponry to bridge the gap with their opponents.	✓
The Vietcong soldiers spoke the same language as the South Vietnamese and shared their culture, which helped them persuade many South Vietnamese to assist them. They were also familiar with the land.	✓
North Vietnamese General Giap was a highly effective general and organiser, who understood how to inspire troops and keep them supplied. He employed the same tactics that he had used to defeat the French.	✓
Members of the US-supported South Vietnamese government were seen as **imperialist puppets**. By contrast, Ho Chi Minh (who died in 1969) and General Giap were seen as Vietnamese heroes who had fought the French and the Japanese.	✓
The USA had to avoid provoking the USSR and China for fear that it might lead to nuclear war. China had developed its own nuclear bombs by 1967.	✓
Guerrilla tactics were very effective in undermining US morale and counteracting the superior numbers and technological advantages of the USA and ARVN.	✓
Communism and the prospect of a fair share of land had significant appeal to poor Vietnamese peasants.	✓
Vietcong troops were highly committed and engaged with the cause, in contrast to many of the US soldiers, who struggled to understand why they were even in Vietnam. Many Vietnamese troops had experience from fighting the French.	✓
The Vietcong were willing to sustain more losses than the USA. US General Westmoreland once remarked that any US General that suffered Giap's losses would have been sacked instantly.	✓
The Vietnamese cause appealed to anti-government protesters in the USA. It was portrayed as a David v. Goliath struggle of Eastern resistance to Western imperialist aggression.	✓

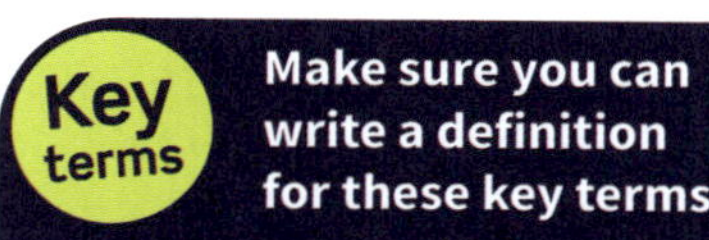

Make sure you can write a definition for these key terms

PTSD imperialist puppet psychedelic

US weaknesses

The North Vietnamese understood and exploited the weaknesses in the US military.

US weaknesses	
The USA struggled with fighting a jungle war, failing to adapt to the harsh conditions. Much of Vietnam was covered with jungle, which was difficult for troops and equipment to get through, and the weather was humid and rainy.	✗
The USA never got to grips with fighting a guerrilla war, which neutralised its technological advantages. The fear of Vietcong booby traps was significant.	✗
US troops were young and inexperienced (the average age of combat troops killed in action was 22).	✗
Many of the drafted soldiers did not want to fight. Morale was low both in Vietnam and at home.	✗
Drugs were available in Vietnam. A 1971 report by the Department of Defense said that 51% of US troops had smoked marijuana, 31% had taken **psychedelics**, and 28% had used hard drugs, such as heroin.	✗
Drafted troops could return to the USA after a year, so the army lost soldiers as they gained experience.	✗
US troops failed to win over the 'hearts and minds' of the South Vietnamese, either to the benefits of capitalism or to South Vietnam's leaders, who were seen as puppets of the US government.	✗
Bombing raids and chemical weapons, as well as the treatment of Vietnamese civilians by the US army, both in general and in extreme cases like at My Lai, further alienated Vietnamese support and made the USA look bad globally.	✗
Vietnamisation failed badly. The ARVN were neither committed nor well-trained enough to hold off the Vietcong without US support.	✗
The perception of the US war effort was seen not as an attempt to contain communism, but as a continuation of French and Japanese imperialism.	✗
The war became increasingly unpopular in the USA. Media and public opinion turned against the war after 1968, making it hard to justify further investment.	✗
The cost of the war was a huge burden on the US economy, leading to spending cuts at home, increased taxes, and inflation.	✗

The impact of opposition to the war in the USA

- Vietnam was the first conflict to be viewed widely from people's living rooms. What was broadcast shamed many Americans and led to increasing distrust of the government.
- Public protests and criticism of the US government grew throughout the 1960s. As opposition to the war mounted, that became harder for the government to ignore. Elected officials could not remain in post for long without popular support.
- Unlike those returning in 1945, at the end of the Second World War, many Vietnam War veterans faced hostility and abuse, as well as discrimination in the workplace, highlighting the deep divisions within US society.

Retrieval

Learn the answers to the questions below, then cover the answers column with a piece of paper and write down as many as you can. Check and repeat until you know them all.

	Questions	Answers
1	What were the main demands of the two sides when peace talks began in Paris in 1968?	The North demanded a halt to all US bombing; the USA wanted a reduction of Vietcong activities in the South
2	When was the Paris Peace Accords signed?	January 1973
3	How long did the Paris Peace Accords give the USA to remove their troops from Vietnam?	60 days
4	When did the communist North formally reunite the country?	2 July 1976
5	How much did the Vietnam War cost the USA?	$168 billion, or $1 trillion in today's money
6	What percentage of the US population served in Vietnam?	More than 1% (one in every 100)
7	What percentage of the surviving soldiers experienced PTSD?	30%
8	Who was the main leader of the North Vietnamese military forces during the war?	General Giap
9	Why did communism appeal to some of the South Vietnamese?	The prospect of land redistribution and the association with national heroes such as Ho Chi Minh and Giap
10	Why did geographical conditions make it difficult for US troops in Vietnam?	Much of the country was covered with jungle that was difficult for troops and equipment to get through; the weather was humid and rainy
11	What problems did returning Vietnam veterans face when back in the USA?	Psychological problems including PTSD; drug addiction; unemployment; marriage break-up; suicide; hostility and abuse as veterans, including discrimination in the workplace

Put paper here

Previous questions

Use the questions below to check your knowledge from previous chapters.

	Questions	Answers
1	Which campaigns did King plan in 1966 and 1967, and which cities did they focus on?	1966: the Chicago Freedom Movement, Chicago; 1967: the Poor People's Campaign, Washington, D.C.
2	What happened to US casualties in Vietnam in the years after Vietnamisation began?	They dropped significantly, from 11 600 in 1969 to just over 2000 in 1971
3	What happened at Kent State University in 1970 that increased opposition to the war?	Four students were shot dead by state troopers during a protest against the Cambodia invasion

Put paper here

Practice

Exam-style questions

Study Source A below and then answer Question 1.

Source A: US sailors and support staff pushing a helicopter off a US ship in the South China Sea to make room for incoming flights filled with evacuees fleeing the Vietcong during the fall of Saigon in 1975.

SOURCE TIP

What sorts of inferences might you draw from a source like this? Ask yourself the following questions:

- What are the people doing and why are they doing it?
- Do they look organised or panicked?
- What might be the cost of their actions?
- Do most of the people look like citizens or military?
- What does the caption tell you? How can that help?

1 Give **two** things you can infer from Source A about the end of the war in Vietnam. **(4)**

Complete the table below to explain your answer.

(i) What I can infer: Details in the source that tell me this:
(ii) What I can infer: Details in the source that tell me this:

2 Explain why the North Vietnamese won the Vietnam War. **(12)**

You **may** use the following in your answer: • the landscape and climate of Vietnam • the tactics of the Vietcong You **must** also use information of your own.

EXAM TIP

Revisit the different causal factors: social, economic, political, cultural, and military. Can you list why North Vietnam won, linked to each factor? What would be a good third reason to choose here?

Great Clarendon Street, Oxford, OX2 6DP, United Kingdom

Oxford University Press is a department of the University of Oxford. It furthers the University's objective of excellence in research, scholarship, and education by publishing worldwide. Oxford is a registered trade mark of Oxford University Press in the UK and in certain other countries.

Written by Mark Stacey

The moral rights of the author have been asserted

First published in 2023

British Library Cataloguing in Publication Data

Data available

978-1-38-204302-1

10 9 8 7 6 5 4 3 2 1

The manufacturing process conforms to the environmental regulations of the country of origin.

Printed in the UK by Bell and Bain Ltd, Glasgow

Acknowledgements
The publishers would like to thank Paul Martin for his work preparing this book for publication.

The publisher and authors would like to thank the following for permission to use photographs and other copyright material:

Photos: p5: Everett Collection Inc / Alamy Stock Photo; **p10:** Associated Press / Alamy Stock Photo; **p14:** winnond / Shutterstock; **p16:** Geopix / Alamy Stock Photo; **p20:** Science History Images / Alamy Stock Photo; **p21(l):** Everett Collection Inc / Alamy Stock Photo; **p21(r):** GRANGER - Historical Picture Archive / Alamy Stock Photo; **p23:** American Photo Archive / Alamy Stock Photo; **p27:** Everett Collection Historical / Alamy Stock Photo; **p31:** Associated Press / Alamy Stock Photo; **p32(t):** Steve Allen / Shutterstock; **p32(m):** blickwinkel / Alamy Stock Photo; **p32(b):** charnsitr / Shutterstock; **p38:** colaimages / Alamy Stock Photo; **p39(t):** patrice6000 / Shutterstock; **p39(b):** Gil C / Shutterstock; **p41:** Everett Collection Historical / Alamy Stock Photo; **p51:** CPA Media Pte Ltd / Alamy Stock Photo

Artwork by Newgen Publishing